Praise for *The* ⸰

"Like a pure mountain spring that comes from deep sources, this book will nourish and refresh you each time you dip into it. Something very special is happening on these pages."

—**Kim John Payne M.ED**, author, *Simplicity Parenting: Using the Extraordinary Power of Less to Raise Calmer, Happier and More Secure Kids*

"We teach children to become successful because we want them to be happy. Harrison turns it around and shows us how to teach children to be happy, alive and connected; prerequisites for engaging in life "successfully." Powerfully written, this is a message that can bring peace and unity to humanity."

—**Naomi Aldort**, author, *Raising Our Children, Raising Ourselves*

"Children are about more than achievement and school. They need to find out who they are and what they like. Harrison's book invites us all to learn about the uniqueness of the children around us and to see the world through their eyes."

—**Roberta Michnick Golinkoff, Ph.D.**, author, *A Mandate for Playful Learning in Preschool* and *Einstein Never Used Flash Cards*

"Harrison wants our kids to grow up joyfully, in love with life and learning. His practical anecdotes give parents and educators the tools to expand and enrich a child's natural development in a world that too often violates these most basic needs. A refreshing, optimistic and practical book."

—**Jane M. Healy, Ph.D.**, author of *Different Learners: Identifying, Preventing and Treating Your Child's Learning Problems*

"This book shows both the challenges we face in truly "educating" our children to a fuller life, but more importantly it shows the universal attitudes and qualities that are essential for bringing out the best in others and ourselves. "

—**Greg Traymar**, Director, Sharing Nature North America

"An inspiring work that comes from the heart through the author's direct experience as a teacher. Harrison has taken the principles of Coyote Teaching and wove them into his personal connection with nature, giving the reader an authentic education where they can then create their own connection to nature and their unique vision that is part of the greater whole. A must read for teachers and parents who are searching for ways to connect children to nature as an answer to 'nature deficit disorder'."

—**Rick Berry**, Founder and Director, 4 Elements Earth Education.

"Simon Harrison affirms that the most important role for parents is to keep that spark in a child's eyes alive. Simon offers practical and profound tools for how to encourage children to be wholly themselves. He gently shows us methods to rekindle lost truths in how we live on earth that allow children to retain and grow their essential humanity. We all must envision a world full of truly alive children!"

—**Nancye Good**, Homeschooling Mom, NYC.

"The Truly Alive Child is a collection of hard earned experiences guaranteed to shake you up and challenge the very foundation of our postmodern society. This is more than a beautiful, educational guide steeped in ancient wisdom. This book is part of a movement and Harrison makes a daring call to action."

—**Matt Abatelli**, Program Director, The Children of the Earth Foundation

"Simon's presence is absolutely enlivening! He is the magnetic current that youth joyously imitate. His passion, sense of humor and Earth-based wisdom are deeply rooted in a soul that is both ancient and genuinely kind. The Truly Alive Child reflects these qualities and holds a rich storehouse of knowledge that will help guide any family to a deeper relationship with the natural world and their own core essence."

—**Craig Rubens**, Long-time Waldorf teacher and Outdoor Educator

The Truly Alive Child

FOR THOSE WHO SEEK A GRANDER
VISION FOR OUR CHILDREN

Simon Paul Harrison

FOX WALKING PUBLISHING
Lyons, Colorado

Printed in the United States of America
Cover and text design by Bookwrights

Publisher's Cataloging In Publication

Harrison, Simon Paul.
The truly alive child: for those who seek a grander vision for our children/Simon Paul Harrison
p.   cm.
Includes index.
LCCN: 2011934855
ISBN-13: 978-0-9834836-2-5
1. Parenting—Religious Aspects.   2. Spirituality—Children.
3. Education—Philosophy.   I. Title.
HQ769.3. H377
649.1

When I was five years old, my mother always told me that happiness was the key to life. When I went to school, they asked me what I wanted to be when I grew up. I wrote down "happy." They told me I didn't understand the assignment, and I told them they didn't understand life.

~John Lennon

Contents

Acknowledgments

I believe that Bob Dylan had it right when he said the answer is "…blowing in the wind." I am grateful this one found me.

I would like to say thank you to all the children whom I have had the good fortune to have learned from and who inspire me to be more.

My gratitude goes out to everyone who has supported me in the writing of this book, particularly Rick Berry, Jorge Brana, Joanna Driver, Steve Catney, Steve Perry, Walt Gigandet, Gabriele Gandswindt, and my wonderful parents, on both sides, for their encouragement, support, and unconditional love. I learn from them every day.

I also thank Tom Brown Jr. and Grandfather Stalking Wolf for guiding me to rediscover my love for life. I hope that this book fulfills a promise I made to them both. They gave me the tools to follow a different path, to move to a different beat. I promised them that if I ever found it I would lead one more person back.

My whole-hearted appreciation goes to my two editors, Arlene Prunkl and Catherine Laurence, and to designer, Mayapriya Long. Their skill and professionalism made them a joy to work with.

Finally I would like to thank my beautiful wife Katherine, for just being who she is.

Introduction

Thank You

Thank you for picking this book up and opening the cover. It means you are conscious that there is so much more we can do and be for our children to allow them to experience being "Truly Alive". I doubt if there has ever been a time of greater urgency in all of human history to ask the question, why is our society not able to create children, teenagers and adults who are indeed, truly alive? Our physical future here on Earth depends on understanding deeply the answer to this challenge. If you choose to read the rest of this book, I thank you for playing a conscious, loving and peaceful role in the lives of children everywhere.

Beliefs

People intrigue me. I am fascinated with observing individuals and society and asking, why? For years, stretching back to my childhood, I wanted to understand deeply what motivates people to do the things they do and why they are the way they are. As a child, I read a book by Richard Scarry called *What People Do All Day* (Random House, 1968) which highlights the many different choices we have before us each day. It planted in me the seeds to continually examine the paths that people's lives take and wonder why people make the choices they do.

When asking about a person's motivation, each answer we discover throws up another question. Like the layers of an onion, as one layer gets peeled away another lies beneath, just waiting to be discovered. Down through these we go until we reach the very core, which for humans is made up of one thing: *beliefs*. We do the things we do and experience life in a certain way because of the beliefs we hold to be true. This is regardless of the extent to which these beliefs agree with reality. Perhaps a good sequel for Richard Scarry's book could be *What People Believe All Day*. The whole of life stems from these beliefs: our perceptions about the world, the way we act, what we do and say, and, for the purposes of this book, how and why we guide children to discover and experience life.

The saying, "You are what you eat" could just as easily read, "You are what you *believe*"! If you believe you are happy, you will probably be happy. Believe you are poor, and life will probably show up like that for you. But then the question arises: *why* do we believe that life is a certain way? The answer, for almost every single person on this planet, is that this is what we have been taught. This is what parents, friends, and particularly society have told us to believe. If we are taught to believe something for almost two decades of our lives, it takes an enormous effort just to question whether it actually true for us, let alone to be able to create something different. This is especially so when everyone else has been taught the same set of beliefs, thereby reinforcing them and making them appear very real. Most of us simply follow what others have told us because that is what is considered "normal"; we have never been taught any different. Our educational systems worldwide play a pivotal role in shaping society and are hugely influential in shaping individuals' beliefs, and thus their very lives. There is a quotation, widely attributed to St. Francis Xavier, that says, "Give me a child until he is seven and I will show you the man." The implication is obviously that the importance of those first years of childhood in shaping the very nature of our lives cannot be underestimated. It is in this developmental period that beliefs, attitudes, personalities, and even our views of reality are all formed. The cake is made, as it were, in those initial years. The icing is added later in life. Thus, a great deal of what we'll explore in this book will be the challenges that the education system has created both for the individual and for society. Life simply cannot be explored without considering deeply the way that children learn about it.

In my early twenties, I understood that the educational system back in my native home of England was not perfect. However, like all teachers when they start out, I wanted to make a difference in the lives of children. I also felt a strong calling to help both individuals and society. So I began my career as an elementary school teacher. It was hard work and could be extremely tiring, but most aspects were immensely satisfying. I loved being around children, watching them grow, and helping them along the path of life.

During this time, the "Why?" questions intensified. I felt, as I still do, that if I could understand children better, get to the core of what makes them tick, I would be able to serve their needs better. Over the period of a few years, these questions became tinged with sadness and at times deep frustration. This was not directed at the children I was teaching, but at the very institution that purports to serve their needs. I could not (and still cannot) educate children in the way I was being asked. To my mind, so much of it was harming children, not helping them. Their natural desires to learn, to explore the world, and to have adventures were leaving them at worryingly young ages. There was so little in the English education system that honored each child as an individual. Instead, the children became points on a graph and positions in a table, taught to compete against everyone else to rise to the top. All this competition was in the name of "success." It seemed to me that the only "success" it achieved was to stamp out a child's creativity and zest for life. I found it too difficult to reconcile my differences with the system I was forced to abide by, and after just over three years, I decided to leave the government-controlled teaching profession.

My desire to help and support children intensified, but I knew it would have to take a different form; I would not have been able to live with myself otherwise. I was offered the opportunity to teach children and families my greatest passion: how to reconnect with nature. My two mentors, Tom Brown Jr. and Rick Berry, showed me a completely different style of education called Coyote Teaching. Similar methods have been used by many indigenous peoples for centuries. Coyote Teaching has been returning to more mainstream culture first through Tom Brown Jr. (www.trackerschool.com) and now also thanks to Jon Young (www.jonyoung.org). It seeks to foster passion in the learner, and is remarkably effective at providing experiences for children that encourage them to become independent, creative beings. For me it was and continues to be fascinating to see that there are a multitude of ways to support a child's development. Through opportunities to learn and work with Tom and Rick, I was extremely fortunate to meet a wide range of children and parents, and to learn about a variety of education philosophies. I worked with homeschooled children, families and adults, regular schoolchildren, and even Boy Scouts. It was a rich experience. I also married into a family of homeschoolers, and they gave me even further insights into the many different worlds of learning.

From Your Heart or From a Report?

"There are lies, damned lies, and statistics," said the British Prime Minister Benjamin Disraeli (allegedly). He meant, of course, that it is easy to manipulate figures to get them to say anything you want. This book does not offer any statistics, latest findings, government reports, or any other facts or figures intended to shock you into action, because our lives should not be dictated by facts and figures. Whenever we reduce the wonder of life to mere statistics, alarm bells should start ringing. Should we seek change, for example, when 37.8 percent of a nation's children fail at exams, or when 24.3 percent of them are clinically depressed? If we stay just below these thresholds, are those children who contribute to the statistic just the accepted "collateral damage"? We like our facts and figures because we can use them to make ourselves "right" and others "wrong." The Internet has proved to be a huge learning tool, because we have masses of information instantly available at our fingertips. However, it also provides us with the information to support our own views, no matter what those views are. You can find research, studies, and figures to back up just about any argument you can conceive of. This book is not an exploration into "right" and "wrong," but instead focuses on the most important measurement: your feelings. I am absolutely certain you do not need government statistics to tell you what your children are feeling, or how those you teach respond to different environments and activities. This book encourages you to create change, not because the latest government report says we should, but because of what you are feeling deep in your heart. The latter is infinitely more powerful than the former.

Is This Book for You?

If you are a parent and you picked up this book because you are seeking a grander life experience for your children, this book is for you. If you are a teacher and are searching for a way to inspire children, this book is for you. And if you are an adult who is looking for ways to create a more loving and peaceful world for children, this book provides the guidance to do that. *The Truly Alive Child* encourages readers to think deeply about the experiences we are putting in front of the next generation. It asks us to become conscious and aware of what we are *doing* and who we are *being* for our children. It provides the means by which a child's life experience and education (the way we learn about life) can be brought into the present moment in a loving and peaceful manner. This can be created not only by parents and teachers, but also by every individual in society. We each have a vital role to play in providing future generations with the kind of life experiences that foster love, peace, joy, and purpose.

You are invited, and given the tools, to find your own truth, to look beyond what we are all being told, far beyond conventional wisdom, and to seek a greater vision. We as adults must ask deep and meaningful questions, because they will show us where and how we can change. But we can only get close to the truth when we are willing to ask questions without deciding the answers beforehand. *The Truly Alive Child* guides us to ask the questions that will lead to real change in the lives of our young ones.

To create an environment for the next generations in which they no longer have to suffer, we must go beyond the limited viewpoint of our current educational and societal systems. To expand our views on education, we must expand our views on life itself. This book provides the framework in which we can join hands with children and walk the path of life together. In harmony, we—both adults and children—can discover who we really are. We can enjoy education, and the experience of being alive, as never before.

The Truly Alive Child explores where we are now, and where we could be if we begin to make certain simple, conscious choices. It looks at our current beliefs and explains how they have come to create an education system and life experience based in fear. Most importantly, it also shows how by changing these beliefs we can create a world that encourages children to be lifelong learners and lovers of life.

The messages contained in this book are like life itself in that everything is interconnected. It is impossible to consider any one thing in isolation. As we keep circling around, it may seem that points are being repeated, but it is like building a house of bricks: the next layer is always being added. As long as we continue to grow, we are moving toward an ever greater understanding of ourselves and the world around us.

This is not a prescriptive book. There are no suggestions for what facts children should learn, or what they should be able to do at certain ages. There are no recommendations on how, for example, we can teach science better or mathematics more efficiently. It is not about how we can squeeze another drop of "progress" out of children. Instead, this book looks deeply into how we can provide an environment for children that encourages them to discover their deepest potential. It provides us with ways in which we can support children in how to be creative, not what to create, and in how to be successful, not what to be successful at.

Children have brought me some of my happiest and most fulfilling experiences. They have led me to a greater understanding of the world around me, and shown me what it is to be truly alive. I hope and pray we can find a way to serve them as life intended: with humility, reverence, and unconditional love.

CHAPTER I

Creating Change

For man, as for flower and beast and bird, the supreme triumph
is to be most vividly, most perfectly alive.

~David Herbert Lawrence

Our Greatest Challenge

Can there be anything in life more sacred, more uplifting or more
perfect than simply watching a young child at play? Children find
eternity in a puddle of mud. They sense wonder in the flutter of a
butterfly's wings. They squeal with delight at the ocean waves chasing
after their feet. They follow the calling of their soul, without question, wherever it may take them, for it is the only guide they need.
They give their love freely and without condition, because they feel
the whole of creation wrapping and embracing them in the safety and
compassion of its bosom. Young children radiate with joy for no ap-

parent reason. It is as if just being alive is cause enough for them to celebrate, to smile deeply with their mouths, their eyes, and their very souls. Anyone who watches closely can see clearly that young children have a deep purpose. They understand profoundly, demonstrated by their actions, that they are free to enjoy their birthright of discovering and experiencing every last nuance of life. As such they are the very definition of being truly alive. It is their natural state of being.

But then, like a thief in the night, their days of enjoying being truly alive seem to slip away, never to return. In truth this way of being never leaves, but it can be forgotten for decades and even lifetimes. It is educated out of them by a system that claims to know what is best, but is so busy congratulating itself and is so horribly addicted to being distracted, that it is blinded to what is actually happening. We may think our society has achieved greatness because it has put a man on the moon or because we are allowed to democratically vote for our leaders, but it cannot even support human beings' most basic desire: to experience our eternal, free nature, one with all of life.

The truly alive child is one who knows intimately who they really are and what their relationship is to life. They know that to play in the puddle of mud is never wasted time, that to marvel at the flight of the butterfly is never mere child's play, and to embrace the cold, wet ocean on their toes is so much more than the just the purely physical act it can appear.

Young children understand, without being taught, that just like them all life is sacred, and that each part of creation has its place, from the largest bear to the smallest ant. They demonstrate their amazing awareness by living their brotherhood and sisterhood with all things, equally and with compassion. They seek not to destroy but to discover, and not to dominate but to love.

Our greatest challenge is so simple it seems almost too easy: to ensure that our natural state of being truly alive never leaves our children. Ever.

A Good Day to Die

"It is a good day to die" is said to have been uttered by many of the Lakota people, a Native American tribe. I have heard it explained that they spoke these words not because they wished to lay down their lives in a fearless charge against the enemy, but because they could say without any doubt that up to that point in their lives, up to that point in the day, they were truly alive. Every moment of their existence from waking to sleeping had been filled to the brim with all that life had to offer.

I remember vividly the very first occasion I could look myself in the eye and speak those powerful words. I can recall the experience as if it were happening right now. It changed my life forever, literally awakening me. My first moment of being truly alive happened with a beautiful fall sunrise, but the story begins the day before.

I was in my mid-twenties and just starting to learn the "old ways," as I now call them. I was taking a course in survival, tracking, and nature awareness with Tom Brown Jr. in the Pine Barrens, a vast wilderness area in southern New Jersey. I knew beforehand what would be expected of me. I had a few days to build myself a debris hut before I would turn in my tent and sleeping bag and allow the Earth to take care of me fully. A debris hut is essentially made up of leaves, pine needles, and other stuff from the forest floor, piled up around a framework of sticks. It should keep you warm, dry, and very content. To most people it is not the Hilton. To me it was heaven.

On the day of my task, I set about making what I hoped would be the world's best first-time debris hut. More than anything I wanted to experience true physical freedom, so I was determined to learn the secret of never needing to carry a tent and sleeping bag with me again. To say I threw myself into my task would be an understatement. By the time I'd finished, the leaf pile was gigantic and looked as though it belonged to some strange and long forgotten woodland creature. I handed in my sleeping bag and tent early. I couldn't wait for it to get dark so I could crawl into my pine-needle palace.

As darkness fell, I stood at the entrance to my new home, hoping that I'd done enough to survive what I knew were going to be freezing temperatures that night. I crawled in and soon fell asleep. I awoke an indeterminate time later with cold legs, cold arms, and frigid air all around me. I realized immediately that I had completely neglected to fill my sleeping chamber with soft, insulating material. Although I knew no better at the time, I was angry with myself for having overlooked such a necessity. I awoke what seemed like every few minutes that night, rubbed my arms and legs, blew on my hands and then tried to sleep some more. After waking up that first time I don't think I could have slept more than an hour for the rest of the night. The last time I awoke, I remember looking up and seeing a chink of light coming through the leaves. My first reaction was to be frustrated for not having plugged that hole in the daytime, something I had known was necessary. Then suddenly, I realized that if light was coming in it must mean—I had survived! The Earth had indeed taken care of me, and I basked in my new definition and experience of freedom. It was morning, and a most welcome one. I pushed out of my debris hut on my belly a few feet until I ended up with my front half out and my back half in, lying propped up on my arms. As I looked around—and I swear it to this day—time stopped right there. Around me the edges of every leaf bore the white tinges of a fall frost and the morning symphony of birdsong and animal activity was just beginning. The sun was pushing through the pine forest, warming my body, and the air was crisp and fresh, invigorating my senses. I could feel the very life-force of the forest flowing around and through me, connecting my soul with that of my brothers and sisters of nature. It was a true moment of oneness, an awakening. I must have said thank you a thousand times to the Earth that I now looked at with new eyes and regarded with new feelings. Every fiber of my being was held in rapture at moving into that larger world. An intimate relationship was revealed to me where I could simultaneously bless life and receive its blessing in return. I whispered, "It is a good day to die," and at last I knew the true meaning of those words. There are some times in your life when you feel like it doesn't matter if you live or die, because you are so blissfully happy, so at peace, and so connected to life that you know you are, in that moment, truly alive.

For me, that was the first moment of true connectedness and awakening, and after that the floodgates opened. I had found my personal path to aliveness—the natural world. Now I experience those same feelings, that same intimate relationship with life as I listen to the wind blow, smell a tree's bark, dip my hand in a mountain stream or watch feeding deer. Millions of us share this nature-connection path to being truly alive because it is so remarkably effective in helping us to understand ourselves and our relationship to life. Close to the Earth, things are real, and so we discover what reality is, and who we really are. We move with the flow of life, not against it.

The path exists for each of us, and is highly individual. But society has us so distracted, so encapsulated in fear, that it can prove our life's greatest challenge even to begin to search for it, let alone walk it.I want to emphasize that I did not just stumble across that first experience of being truly alive. It was the result of at least seven years of personal torment, anguish, self-doubt, paralyzing fear, anger and frustration. We should be clear that the path to being truly alive does not require these battles in order to earn some badge of honor, allowing us to "pass" through to the other side. My suffering was very much self-inflicted through my resistance to my old, ill-informed models of life. I made the choice to let go, or unlearn my old models very slowly: hence seven years of pain. At every step of the journey I felt it would be far easier to give in and return to "normality". Yet no matter what I did, a voice deep inside me would not stop urging me toward my personal path of aliveness. I could hear it, and I knew full well it spoke the truth, but almost every fiber of my being fought against it. To seek the kind of adventures it was urging me toward went against almost everything I had been taught by the education system and by society, whose ideas of success came first at that time in my life. A good job (which I considered myself to have as an elementary school teacher), a good salary, benefits, and prospects for future success were all mine. In most people's view I was safe, secure and comfortable. But still that little voice spoke to me. It may have been quiet, but it was incredibly strong. Every time I didn't occupy my mind with some distraction, in it would jump. I tried television, alcohol, relationships, vacations, video games, promotion at work, and spending money, all in a vain effort to make it go away. In the end, I could no longer stand myself, and so I gave in to that voice that was urging me to follow my heart and, through adventures close to the Earth, seek the truth of who I really was. It was the single best decision I have ever made in my life.

We are born being truly alive, so why should we then inflict a society and an education system on our children that sees us regress into a smaller, more violent, fearful and even cruel reality? Do we really need, as I did, to have to hit rock bottom in order to begin to seek the path home to peace and joy? Do we have to wait until we have a mid-life crisis before we return to the basics of love and purpose beyond the self? Naturally, we all know we do not, but right now that merry-go-round—our creation—is spinning awfully fast and we've got to be either very brave or have nothing to lose to jump off.

And what about our children? What if, early in their lives, we didn't put them on that merry-go-round in the first place? What if they didn't have to fight against the demons that have been planted in their minds through the myths we perpetuate to them?

We can lead our children back to being truly alive, but it will take vision and willpower. It will take love and humility and the strength to believe in ourselves and our children. Most of all it will take a conscious effort for us all to create a new world, and a grander reality.

I cannot think of any greater motivation in the universe than making sure not even a single child grows up without finding their path to experiencing being truly alive.

Creating Change

It is likely you picked up *The Truly Alive Child* because you want to make a real difference in the lives of children. You are not alone. Children have a special place in all our hearts. It seems almost impossible to put into words the joy we experience watching young children at play; it is as if their happiness and laughter speak to our very soul. They are able to capture our imagination unlike anything or anybody else. They can bring out the best in us as we seek to protect their childhood innocence and help them develop and maintain their love for life. Adults the world over agree that our children deserve the very best.

Yet, however noble our goals and dreams are, we so often fail to turn them into a reality that children actually experience. Why should this be so? Is it because we all find it hard to agree on what is actually best? Or is it because people in positions of power who have the ability to influence many lives are lacking in vision? These are just two examples of many "blame" scenarios that rob us of our power to create change.

Both of these would be wrong because they buy into the voice of our small self. The small self can only exist in a world of separation and superiority which, as we shall see in the coming chapters, are two of the most powerful illusions humans have created. We are so much more than we think, and it is only by discovering and embracing our true, full identity that we can serve children the way life intended— with humility, reverence and unconditional love.

Guiding children to the greatest gift life can offer—*experiencing who they really are*—gives us all hope that we can create a better tomorrow. We can do so by discovering and living a series of life-changing beliefs that we can give to children as gifts. These gifts are not necessarily tangible. A child could not sit in wide-eyed anticipation as we enter the room with these gifts in a large, wrapped box. They could not tear off the wrapping, reach inside, and hold up the gifts for all to see. Yet these gifts of intangible beliefs are more powerful than any of our human-made creations. They are more powerful than our technologies, our governments and our corporations because they have the ability to change reality in an instant. They can and do change the world, and there are no prerequisites for being able to give them other than being who we are.

It does not matter whether you are rich or poor, what the color of your skin is, whether you are male or female, young or old, or any other label you care to think of. If you are alive and breathing, you have these gifts to give. They are inside us all, and so they are with you, right now, just waiting for you to call upon them. They never, ever leave you, because they *are* you.

You, like every other individual on this planet, have the power to create a different world and life experience for children. It doesn't need all seven billion of us to agree. Nor are we reliant on the governments and corporations of the world to do something for us. The difference that one individual can and does make is truly staggering. It can be life-changing. And that is surely what you are reading this book for—to change a child's life.

Many Paths Lead to the Mountain Top

It is not for one soul to judge and claim they know what is best for any other. The concepts and ideas throughout this book are simply observations; there is no judgment behind them. I am not saying it is "wrong" or "bad" to do or think certain things, or that some choices are superior to others. When we start passing judgments and applying labels such as "good" and "bad" we can easily become angry and righteous, which leads to us fighting both with ourselves in our own minds and with our fellow humans. This is the last thing any of us needs.

If you want to purchase a new pair of shoes but are searching for them in a florist's, it is not a judgment if someone informs you that you will not find any in there. Similarly, when reading "should" and "must" in the chapters that follow, remember that they are simply signposts toward providing environments for children in which they can be truly alive, experiencing an abundance of love, peace, joy, and purpose. There are many other choices. It is important to acknowledge that one choice can never be superior to any other, or the only way possible. Many roads lead to the top of the mountain. However, certain choices work better or are more effective in creating certain desired outcomes. For example, if we want children to grow up experiencing deep peace, it really does not work to continually subject them to images of violence. I am simply making an observation of the outcomes that arise from certain choices and actions. If we truly desire change for our children, we must look at all the options before us, with love and respect, and then decide what our highest and grandest choice will be. It is up to each of us to decide what our truth is, and then to live it, consciously and creatively.

We Are in Need

Our global society is short on a great many things, but we are particularly in need of what could be considered the four basics of life: love, peace, joy, and purpose.

Love. We are short not only on love for the creatures of our planet, but we are lacking in love for life itself. We are unable to give unconditional love, always wanting or expecting something in return. Our families and communities are changing before our eyes, becoming ever more fragmented, isolated, and destructive. Where do modern children find real love amidst this continual separation from life?

Peace. There can be no hiding from the cold hard truth that we are short, desperately so, on peace. Humankind's actions are remarkably violent. Worse still, we are accustomed to it on a daily basis, and have learned to justify our violence because we are the ones who are "right," and others "wrong". For the individual there is little inner peace. Our minds are constantly running through the worries of tomorrow and re-living our regrets of the past. Where do children find any kind of peace? All too often our modern world overpowers our senses with artificial stimuli and keeps us locked in small, separate worlds that do nothing for our health. Do children find peace from life around them? Not usually, because they are taught to compete against it. Instead, they have to escape reality and seek solace in films, television, and video games.

Joy. Most individuals lead lives of quiet desperation with true joy coming only in rare, fleeting moments. Mostly we fantasize about the joy we might be able to reach in the future, never actually experiencing it in the present moment. We usually need a good reason to shake us into being happy because, for most of us, simply being alive is not enough. Where do children find joy? In many cities, suburbs and communities they do not seem to play outside anymore. They are encapsulated in air-conditioned buildings, cut off from all their sources of sheer delight such as catching frogs, building shelters in the woods, and riding bikes until dark. Do video games, the Internet, or cell phones bring the same depth of joy as these real, old-fashioned favorites?

Purpose. We are lost. It is no use claiming otherwise because our actions speak louder than our words. Purpose in life for most people is about surviving their time on Earth through gritted teeth. Right now in modern society we do not understand what it means to lead lives of deep and meaningful purpose, especially beyond the self. For children who are rapidly becoming adults, what is their purpose? What drives them to want to be better every day, to seize the moment, and to live life to the fullest? Many teenagers are so horrified by the adult world that they want nothing to do with it whatsoever. They rebel for as long as they can before in their eyes they "sell out" and join in the mindless living, alongside everyone else.

Love, peace, joy, and purpose. These are the four states of being that are continually referred to in this text because they lead to a life that is *free*, and a life that is *full*. What else is there? If these states of being were with us and our children in every waking moment, what more would we need in order to be truly alive? These four states of being are all interconnected and are crucial to the lives we say we want to provide our children with. Along with fear, they are the primary motivating factors behind all human actions. Everyone makes decisions because they hope a particular choice will increase one or more of the four positive states. Enter into a relationship: find an increased level of *love*. Go for a walk in nature: feel an increased sense of *peace*. Play a game: increase feelings of *joy*. Change a job: find an increased sense of *purpose*.

It is fair to say that almost every single person on this Earth yearns and aches to experience more of these, every single day. Yet all too often we find so very little. Love comes only fleetingly, and peace is shattered soon after it is found. Joy happens for a few brief moments a day, and purpose for most people is about surviving, not thriving. Without a doubt, they should all be at the center of our human experience, not something we grasp at on the periphery. Everything should, and can, emanate from an abundance of these. As soon as we become conscious and aware of the choices we are making, the shift will be inevitable.

Children Live What They Are Taught

We live the beliefs we are taught as children by our parents, society, and especially by our educational establishments. The beliefs we learn shape us as adults and go on to shape our own children. For better or worse, the power and influence that these three groups have should not be underestimated. They quite literally tell us what our reality and life experiences will be.

Every moment of the day, children are like sponges, absorbing everything they see and hear. They then simply reproduce in their actions what they see in the world around them. We should be grateful that children act as a mirror for adults, and for society as a whole. They show us the whole picture we are creating, not just the pieces we choose to acknowledge. If we are able to look deeply, with an open heart and mind, we will learn all we need to make meaningful, compassionate change.

If our children are behaving violently, it is because we have taught them to be violent. If our children are fearful, it is because we have taught them to be fearful. If our children are unhappy, it is because we have taught them to be unhappy. If our children lack purpose, it is because we have given them no reason to search for any. Naturally, no teacher or parent deliberately instructs a child to be violent, unloving or unhappy. Yet we are responsible, every single one of us, for all that we pass on to children—both that which serves them in being truly alive, and that which does not. It is not only our schools and teachers that have an influence on our children's experience. It is also our very culture—society itself. It informs our education system, controlling the direction it takes, deciding how our current beliefs and values will be passed to the next generation. So we have a "chicken and egg" situation. Society is formed by how we are educated, and we are educated according to what society believes and values. Therefore, education and society are the two pillars that play the pivotal roles in our life experiences. One creates the other, which creates the other, and a circle is established and then ingrained.

If indeed we seek real change, to provide lives of love, peace, joy, and purpose for the next generation, we must begin to truly acknowledge what we see. If we take an honest, open look at society, we can only conclude that the way we are educating is simply not producing these outcomes. We live in a paradise but are educating children as if we live in a hell. We are teaching them that this is a world in which they should constantly be fearful. We have moved so far away from teaching simple things like our four basic states of being (love, peace, joy, and purpose) that we don't know which way to turn. Politicians, teachers, and parents alike are all looking to one another for answers. "What can we do?" is the question to which we are desperate to find answers. "What can we do so our children won't fail?"

Because we are beginning to acknowledge that our current way of doing things is just not working, we have the perfect opportunity to ask a new set of deep and far reaching questions, the answers to which will help us choose a different path in the way we support children in their interactions with life. People all over the world are beginning to understand on a deeper level that it is time to change, if not for ourselves, then for our children.

There is possibly no stronger force in the universe than the love that adults have for children. Almost every adult wants the absolute best for the next generation. We go to extraordinary lengths and make remarkable sacrifices in our own lives in order to put our children first. None of us would willingly accept an educational system that harms our children in any way. But we have all been walking the same path for so long that it has become a rut that now runs so deep we are unable to see over the sides to a different world. We must climb out of this prison of our own making and look around. It is time to think outside the box. There is no use having one side of the argument saying we should test children at eleven years old and the other side saying it should be sixteen. Similarly, it is pointless having one side favoring class sizes of thirty children, and the other side favoring ten. All of these arguments are so shortsighted they are painful—in some cases, literally.

If, after reading this book, you are still in doubt about how we are unconsciously damaging children with our beliefs and actions, please, take the time to discover and understand what is true for you. In fact I urge you not to just take my word for it. After reading this book, volunteer at a local school. Observe objectively. Consider if the experiences children are receiving will lead them to be truly alive. And do the same with the other pillar: society. Ask yourself honestly if children's environments and the messages they hear on a daily basis are conducive to setting up a young life that will be full of love, peace, joy, and purpose.

Like so many adults, I dream of a day when every single child lives in a place of unconditional love. A day when their very nature is to be peaceful, and the world around them is at peace. When joy is with them in each waking moment and they have a life purpose that is deep and enriching. Maybe this dream sounds too far-fetched, but I think it is not. Maybe other dreamers feel they are alone in their vision, but again, I think they are not.

Millions of people have the same dream, but do not know how or where to begin. We can start by looking honestly at the environments we currently place children in and begin asking questions, without deciding the answers in advance. And not easy ones such as how we can get children to read at ever earlier ages. We must ask deep, soul-searching questions, which I understand can be challenging. Who am I? Why am I here? Why are we educating children? What experience does this choice lead to? How do these choices affect children? We can constantly ask "Why?" and begin peeling through the layers of education until we arrive at the most basic beliefs we choose to pass on to children.

Asking deep questions about our own actions is not something that comes easily for most individuals and certainly not for society. Every single one of us has things we prefer not to think about or to stir up because it can cause us pain. However, if I suffer from recurring headaches, I have a number of choices. First, put up with the pain for the rest of my life and accept that as part of my world. Second, take a pill each time it happens to numb the pain and ignore what my body is telling me. Or third, start asking why, finding out what is causing them, and then make changes to reach a more positive experience. To change this world we must be the ones who choose this last option. We must find out why we are causing ourselves and others so much pain, even if that means we are uncomfortable or uneasy in the short-term. One of the greatest challenges our society faces is the ability to ask questions *without deciding the answers in advance.* Our children and grandchildren are waiting to find out what our choice will be. Will we do what we have always done, thereby getting what we have always got, or will we find the strength and courage to lead our children to be truly alive?

CHAPTER 2

Back To Basics

There is no greatness where there is not simplicity.

~Leo Tolstoy

What Will We Feed?

There is a Cherokee story of an old man teaching his grandson about life. "A fight is going on inside me," he said to the boy. "It is a terrible fight between two wolves. One is evil—he is angry, greedy, and arrogant. He lies, destroys and is full of ego. The other is good—he is joyful, loving, serene, humble, truthful and compassionate. The same fight is going on inside you—and inside every other person too." The young boy thought about these words for a moment and then asked his grandfather, "Which wolf will win?" The old Cherokee simply replied, "The one you feed."

To create real change we have to think, act, and immerse ourselves in a different world. We have to choose which world we will
feed and give energy to, every moment, every day. Right now children
hear the exact opposite of love, peace, joy, and purpose. They are
immersed in a world where they hear that life is full of fear, violence,
sadness and cruelty. The media brings us news every day that human beings are killing other human beings. Some of these killings
may seem to be justified, such as when we go to war. Others, such as
cold-blooded murder, do not. Thus, children, who are all very intelligent, learn that in some instances, killing another human is not only
normal, but also actually encouraged. Television, movies, and video
games routinely show violence and anger as normal human traits.
We are overwhelmed every day by commercials telling us we lack
something in our lives: cosmetic products to make us more attractive,
financial products to keep us secure, gadgets to save us time, electron-
ics to help us relate to others, and an infinite number of things that
will bring us the happiness we so crave. We demonstrate to children
every day that we consider ourselves superior to all other forms of life
as we destroy the Earth and many of its inhabitants. Children absorb
all this information and it is only natural they conclude there must
be a huge number of things to be worried and fearful about. It would
be bad enough if these teachings were just confined to adult society,
but the education system that is teaching children every day uses fear
as its prime motivating factor. The next generation is constantly being taught that the only way to escape from this fear is to succeed in
education: get good qualifications, get a good job, rise to the "top," and
you won't have quite so many things to worry about going without.
Our world is only like this because we unconsciously feed and create
it with our thoughts, our words, and our actions. We can look at our
creations, shrug our shoulders and turn away, because, "That's just
the way it is". Or we can realize that if we created one world we can

certainly create another, but this time consciously, with love and with care. With understanding and compassion. With our children, and for our children.

Changing Gently

As a global society, we have learned so much in a very short period. In all aspects of life, great changes have occurred over the past half century. New understandings in all walks of life have given us much hope for the future of humankind. Every day, we are discovering that life is far grander than we previously imagined it to be. It is time we had a manner of educating children in alignment with our new beliefs and understandings of how full and magnificent life is.

Consciously creating change to give children more freedom, more adventure, and more love, joy and peace can be challenging. Not for children, but for us adults. But it's okay; we can trust our children. They are capable of much more than we think. For every ounce of love and freedom we show them, they will give back many, many times over.

Just because something is challenging does not mean we should seek an easier path. There is no "almost as good" alternative to love. There is no acceptable substitute for freedom. The path is challenging to us only because we have ignored it for so long. Lao Tzu, the Chinese philosopher, said, "A journey of a thousand miles begins with a single step." Can we, as individuals and as a society, take that first step to gently guiding children back to a life that is overflowing with love, peace, joy, and purpose?

As we take these steps, one by one, we should seek change by matching the journey and the destination, by *being* what we want to teach. We must teach love by being loving, not by using fear and anger to achieve the goal. We should teach peace by being peaceful, not by using violence to show how peace-loving we are. We must teach joy by being joyful, not by making a conditional promise in the future ("If you achieve such and such, then you and I will be happy"). We must teach purpose by living a purposeful life, not by using hollow words to set unachievable goals. The journey is where life in all its glory is actually experienced.

It is okay for us to be gentle with ourselves—in fact, we must be. Gentleness holds great power. Look at the mountain stream that trickles slowly downward, but cuts its way through seemingly unbreakable rock. It is slow and steady, yet unrelenting. Change on the scale that sees dramatic differences in our children's life experiences is not going to be instantaneous. We must avoid the sweeping statements of change that so often prevent sweeping change from happening. We have all made them. "I'm going to work out five times a week from now on." Inevitably, the change of lifestyle lasts indeed for just one week. To change in the way that our children need, we must do so gently, from moment to moment. It is far easier to make numerous small changes that add up to great change rather than one huge leap. Later, as we look back, we will see how far we have come. Or, to put it another way, we will see what we have *become*.

Changing gently also means being proud of who we are in each moment. Just because we are aiming to create something different for children does not mean we are failing until we "get there." The mountain stream is not "failing" until it reaches the sea, it is succeeding magnificently at every inch of its journey.

All of the things that our children need are found in the present moment. They are not found grasping and groping at a future that is constantly out of our reach. Equally we must be gentle with ourselves about our past. We all have things that with hindsight perhaps we would have done differently, but what merit is there in re-living these constantly in the present? We are not who we were yesterday. We are who we are today. We can all be proud to say that right now, given our understandings of the world, we are doing the very best we can.

Parents are doing the very best they can for children. Teachers are doing the very best they can, and schools and communities are doing the very best they can as well. We can be proud of the world we have created, yet in the same breath we can also acknowledge that it does not represent our new understandings, desires and beliefs, and that we wish to create something new. We can now consciously choose for ourselves and for our children to be something different. Each day we can choose to be the best and grandest version of love, peace, joy, and purpose that our beliefs will allow.

By being gentle with ourselves in how we create a new life experience for our children, we will be like the stream flowing through the mountains—perfect in every moment, yet ever changing.

Our Birthright

If you only had one day with a child, what would you do, what would you teach, what would you say, where would you go, how would you act, and what would you expect from them?

If you had just one day to spend with a child, what would be the most important things for you to pass on? Would you teach them about mathematics, science, how to fly-fish, or how to ask questions? Would you spend time on history, reading, how to play music or the importance of critical thinking? The list is endless. There are no right or wrong answers here, just choices. What would your choice be? In such a short span of time, some things that we currently place great importance upon might not seem so crucial. Others, currently of little value to us, might gain great significance.

One day? That is not enough time to share with children everything that's important to us. It is not enough time to pass all of our knowledge on to them, and it certainly is not enough time to teach them how to do everything. However, we each have beliefs we hold dear to us that we hope to be able support our children with. So we must start by discarding things until we are left with just a small handful that represent our life's most basic hopes and dreams. We would surely want to share these so that our children are able to be these and more in their own lives. The hopes and dreams we would share in that short time are what we consider our *birthright* to be. In other words, even if nothing else happens in their lives, we will do our very best to ensure a child's birthright is met. I have asked many people what they consider this to be. No two answers have been the same, but they have included simply to be happy, to experience a natural connection with the Earth, and to choose one's own life path.

I believe it is every child's birthright to be who they really are: a beautiful, creative, eternal soul, connected to all of life. I would urge you to consider very deeply your own vision of every child's birthright. You cannot be wrong, so don't worry about giving the "correct" answer. However, consider very carefully whether that birthright dictates to children or frees them. Does it promote love or fear? If you had only the present moment—right here, right now—what would you tell a child their birthright is?

Of course, it really doesn't matter if you have one hour, one day, or fifty years. Cutting down the time to just one day forces us to focus on the present moment. We tend to think of having unlimited amounts of time to download information onto children. Or, to put it more accurately, we have unlimited tomorrows, an unlimited amount of future that we can dream about. But you cannot *be* anything in the future, and you cannot *be* anything in the past. That is because before and after exist only in our minds, not in reality. Right now is all that exists. If we are to help our children to be truly alive, it can only happen in the present moment. This concept seems so simple, but it is not an overstatement to say it changes everything.

Drew's Story

One summer in New Jersey, while I was working at a primitive skills and nature school, we set the teenaged participants an awesome challenge. Our program was all about living in nature invisibly, finding our boundaries, and pushing beyond what we thought were our physical and spiritual limits. The teenagers had one hour to run off into the woods, make a fire by primitive means (by rubbing two sticks together), cook their dinner, hide the fire, camouflage themselves, and find a hiding place before we, the staff, would come to "hunt" them with water balloons.

After the hour was up, the staff, armed with water balloons, set off to find them. As you would expect, the woods were quiet and still. The young people had chosen ingenious hiding places, and were utterly silent. The hide-and-seek element of the game lasted for a further hour, and by the end of it we had found almost all the hiding places the teenagers had chosen. Darkness was falling, so we called everyone in. It was quite a sight, about thirty people, all covered in mud and leaves, emerging from the woods. In the dusk, it was easiest to see people from their shining white teeth. The scene was animated, with people milling about, telling and listening to stories of last-second escapes, near misses, and balloons bursting on heads. As I walked around, I noticed one of the older teens, Drew, standing quietly on the periphery of things, a contented smile on his face. I approached him and asked him how his experience was, thinking he would tell a similar story to everyone else. "I realize now that's the first time I've ever been truly alive," he said. Naturally I asked what he meant. "It was the first time in my life that I was just living in the present moment. Nothing else existed, just me—waiting, watching, listening. I don't remember actually thinking about anything, I was just aware. That was amazing." I have very rarely seen a person so full of joy and peace as Drew was that evening, as if his happiness could not be shaken no matter what happened around him. His answer taught me so much, and continues to teach me every day. I am very grateful to have been around Drew's life-changing moment that summer's evening in New Jersey.

From Doing to Being

Education and life exist only in the present moment, not in some Alice in Wonderland, forever-just-out-of-reach experience. Education should exist—should just *be*—all around us; it is the essence of life itself. All we are really doing when we educate is guiding children to understand and experience life. This means we should no longer sustain an educational culture that is simply *doing*. It must become *being* education. Instead of teaching children how to do spelling and mathematics, remember facts, and pass tests, we should provide a life education for children that emphasizes *being*. Being loving, peaceful, joyful, and full of purpose. Children would in all likelihood still do spelling and mathematics, but these would only happen because of what they are being. If a child is being happy and that leads them to do mathematics, they are well on the way to a rich experience.

Ours is currently a *doing* education system because, for example, children do mathematics in order to be successful. Happiness, if one works hard enough, is a possible by-product, not a conscious choice. I did this in my own life. When choosing my university course, I made my decision purely based on what I could do well, and as a result what I hoped would bring me the most external success. In my mind this was represented by working a successful career on the stock exchange and earning a high salary, and, to be honest, not a lot else.

Not surprisingly, my university experience was excruciatingly boring. I turned off and away from what I was being in the present moment, sacrificing my love for learning in exchange for a distant goal that mercifully never materialized. It took me a number of years to want to voluntarily put myself in a position to learn anything again. I don't regret any of this now, but it pains me to think of teenagers and young adults who are making choices based on the same assumptions as we speak. In the new education paradigm we so desperately need, we would encourage children to make a conscious choice of the state in which they wish to *be* first—for example, being happy—and allow their choice of what to *do* to flow from there.

Martin Luther King Jr. said, "Peace is not merely a distant goal that we seek, but a means by which we arrive at that goal." In other words, we should encourage our children to be at peace, and peaceful action will follow.

One of the greatest gifts we can give to the next generation is the gift of freedom to be alive in the present moment. Children can be whatever they choose. Doing has limits, but being is unlimited. Once we teach children how to *be*, we provide them with a lifetime of possibilities in the present moment. From this, real education and a full life experience are born.

CHAPTER 3

Embracing the Real Child

For my ally is the Force … Life creates it, makes it grow.
Its energy surrounds us and binds us … you must feel the
Force around you; here, between you, me, the tree, the rock,
everywhere, yes.

~Yoda, from *Star Wars*

The Real Jake

A number of years ago, I had the pleasure of spending a few weeks with a family that attended one of our nature-based programs. The mother, Karen, brought her two sons—Ryan, six, and Jake, twelve. It is fair to say that Jake was not the calmest of children, and, while not falling behind academically, he was struggling in a number of areas.

Karen had brought him to see if some time in nature would help him at all.

We had two adventure-packed weeks. We swam in the lake, told stories and ate around the camp fire, played games, and discovered the secrets of nature. By the time he left, Jake was noticeably calmer and more focused, but nothing could have prepared me for how much of a change his time reconnecting to nature brought about when he returned home.

I saw Karen again around nine months later, and she was bursting with excitement to tell me what Jake had been up to. Karen explained to me how, one evening early into the fall term following the summer nature program, she had pressed him to remember his ten spellings for the next day's test. Jake answered almost flippantly that he knew them all. Karen found this hard to believe, simply because he had never got more than three or four out of ten before, so she tested him on his spellings. She was amazed to find that, not only did he indeed know all ten of his words, but he had even learned some extra ones. Astounded, she asked Jake how he had done it. Jake explained that after he had heard one of the stories we told at camp about everything in nature being alive and connected, he knew it could help him. So, at twelve years old, he had chosen to experience himself as being connected to the woods. He said that when he needed to learn he just concentrated on trees, asking them for extra energy, and it was this that helped him achieve his first ten out of ten on the spelling test. Karen didn't question this, but asked him how this would work if he were sitting in a classroom with no access to trees. Again, completely unfazed, Jake had explained to her how distance didn't matter—all he had to do was know he was connected. Karen, with tears in her eyes, told me, "He just said it as if it was the most natural thing in the world." Jake is still full of energy, but the quality of the new positive energy is almost tangible. Like Karen and her family, I have not yet stopped learning from Jake's remarkable insight.

Body, Mind, and Soul

At this point, before we start exploring the finer details of reconnecting with life, it is important to uncover the most basic foundation stone that will transform children's life experience, bringing about love, peace, joy, and purpose as never before. It is wonderfully simple, but at the same time can be supremely complex, depending on how we look at it.

Beliefs are the foundation from which our lives grow. The kinds of beliefs we harbor and their strength shape our choices and actions. For example, if you believe that children benefit in many different ways from having a pet, you will probably encourage your children to care for an animal. If you do not have this belief, your children having pets will probably be of little importance to you. Pretty simple!

A crucial belief we must explore and share with children is that we, along with all living things, are multi-part beings. Labels are unimportant, but for the purposes of this book we will use the terms *body*, *mind*, and *soul* to describe the three parts that make us up. It is open to each of us to use whatever terms feel right for us and our children.

It is most important for us to explore and share this belief with children because the current educational "wisdom" is that we are simply body and mind. It neglects that third part, the soul, and so it is incomplete. Because we do not acknowledge the soul, we do not believe in it. Because we do not believe in the soul, we do not teach about it. Because we do not teach about it, we do not experience it. Finally, because we do not experience it we do not acknowledge that it exists. The circle of negation is complete, but the life experience of children is not.

While it is generally accepted that we have a body and a mind, it is the concept of the soul that brings up some contention. For some it is preposterous. For others it is a way of life, as real as breathing in and out. Some people have called it the higher self, or the spirit. I believe it is *connectedness*—the part of us that is connected to all things. Our soul joins with all others to make up the energy that is *God*, the *Creator*, the *Is*, the *All*, the *Great Spirit*, the *Universe*, the *Force*, the *Tao*. Again, the labels are unimportant. I am using the term *soul* to describe the part of us that is mostly forgotten, but will never leave. It is waiting patiently to be acknowledged. And, when it is, our children will never be the same again. For when we experience that we are a soul, that we are more than we have ever imagined, connected to all things, a life of love, peace, joy, and purpose is virtually inevitable.

Our soul is the highest love. It is the greatest peace. It is joy beyond comprehension, and its purpose is simply to *be*. The world that the soul moves in is far, far larger and more complex and powerful than the world our physical bodies belong to. It offers us a fuller, grander experience, and the opportunity, through its depths, to be truly alive. However, and this is vitally important, we should not seek to abandon the body and the mind in favor of the soul. It would be wise of us to educate and support children to experience all three in balance, otherwise we meet one challenge and create another!

Truth is revealed to us in many forms, and not always in the way we would expect. Who would have thought that a small, elderly green alien called Yoda could guide us toward a great truth? But that is exactly what he does in the *Star Wars* films by teaching Jedis about the *Force*. The idea that the Force "surrounds us and binds us" is put forward by Yoda to explain that all things are connected. It is a consciousness, just as you are consciously reading these words, or as I am writing them. It is alive, flowing through us and in us, through animals, forests, flocks of birds, bodies of water, mountain ranges, and even through society. It can easily be felt, as tangible as the book you are holding right now, but this is only possible when we live in balance, with an inner peace and trust for life. When we let go of fear, the soul becomes like a flower opening its petals to the warmth of the sun. We can finally be who we really are, a beautiful being, shining with confidence and creativity.

When I was a teenager, just beginning to ask questions and un-learn some things I had been taught by mainstream society, I had the good fortune to attend a talk by a Canadian man, Ron, about how he had turned his life around from the depths of despair to daily rapture simply by acknowledging his connectedness to all things. It was a very small group with probably no more than fifteen people in atten-dance, so, being a curious and somewhat skeptical teenager, I took the opportunity to ask him how he knew for sure what he was espousing was true. He walked with me outside to a garden pond and told me to put my hand in it. I humored him and plunged my hand in. "Is the water wet?" he asked me. I laughed and answered that obviously it was. "How do you know?" he then asked. In my mind I continued to laugh at the ridiculousness of the question. The answer was simple: "Because I can feel it." Ron just smiled and said, "So can I."

There is no separation; nothing exists in isolation. It doesn't mat-ter how advanced our technology becomes, how many computers, lasers, or particle accelerators we produce, the doorway into the world of the soul will always be the same: through our feelings.

We Are All One

At some point, on some level, one that right now most people are unaware of, our lives are intertwined. They are intertwined and con-nected, not only to one another as humans, but also to every single thing in the universe. By intertwined, I don't mean that what we do directly or even indirectly affects everything else, but that we are liter-ally connected. Put more simply, we are all made of the same stuff, and each bit of stuff is connected to everything else. Picture the ocean. Is it one big body of water, or is it billions of tiny droplets of water all joined together? The answer is—it is both. It just depends on which way you look at it. We are like the droplets in the ocean. We are all individual, but we are also all connected.

The idea that we are all connected is not new. It has been repeated for centuries, and over time many different labels have been given to the energy where all things come together, including *God, Creator, Usen* (a Native American term), the *Great Spirit*, the *Life*, the *Is, Oneness*, the *Force*. However, the label is unimportant; the truth and the experience are crucial.

If we can accept that we are interconnected with all of life in a vast sea of energy, it becomes easy to see that, where it all comes together, there is only one. But, just like the ocean, the *one* is composed of many different parts, each with its own individual consciousness. "We are all *one*" has been said by many, for decades and even centuries, and it is one of the most basic truths of life.

The belief and experience that we are all one has profound implications for the way we perceive the world. For many it leads to lives of great love because it brings about the experience of being safe and secure. There is no judgment meted out by this one soul, so there is complete freedom to explore and discover life. For others there is a wonderful feeling of peace—a feeling of everything being in perfect order or "at home," no matter what might happen on life's path. When this truth is embraced, it changes an individual's beliefs concerning life, in particular about the reason we are here. If we are serious about creating love, peace, joy, and purpose for the generations to come, the basic tenet that we are all one has to be at the very core of our beliefs and, by extension, our education systems. It should represent both the end of the line, and the first foundation stone. It should be where our teachings stem from and where they return to. It shifts the focus from "get through with gritted teeth," which many millions of people experience on a daily basis, to a glorious, lifelong experience of self-discovery. When life is lived believing and experiencing that we are all one, the doorway is permanently open to our long neglected friends: love, peace, joy, and purpose.

If there were only you in the world, there would be no one else to fear, and you could not fear yourself. Do you fear your own right leg? Of course not. It will never harm you, and you will never deliberately harm it. If there were only you in the world, there would be no one else to compete against, and you could not compete against yourself. Do you compete against your left arm? Again, of course not. You can't be superior to your left arm, and your left arm can't be superior to you. It is you, and you are it. Of course, the size of the analogy is unimportant. It doesn't matter if we are talking about your body, or all the beings in the Universe. There is only *one*. We are all connected, all together. When we experience that we do not have to be fearful, we can be loving. When we experience that we do not have to compete, we can be peaceful. When we experience that we do not have to worry, we can be joyful. And when we experience that we are never, ever lost, for we are everywhere and everything, we can be purposeful.

Until we are willing to embrace the idea that we are all one, there will be no significant change in the way we educate our children and the lives we lead them into. All our other attempts to change rest on a purely physical level, and as such they merely scratch the surface of any problems we see. Right now, the conditions in our world mirror our ideas about our own being. Most people do not believe they are a soul as well as a body and mind. This leaves our life experiences very unbalanced. It is the lack of belief in and experience of a soul that is connected to all things that is creating this seemingly cruel world. Because our understanding of life is incomplete, we create an incomplete life experience and education system for both ourselves and the next generation.

I would urge everyone who wishes to share their passions with children to explore or at least entertain the idea that we each have a soul that is connected to all things. We do not have to be spiritual masters or understand every nuance of our being. If we can simply acknowledge the possibility that there is a door marked "Soul," I am confident our children will walk through it faster than we could ever imagine. Let us allow children the space to find, discover, and enjoy their soul *freely* and *fully*. This is truly a gift.

For anyone who might like a little more information from our current culture to test the waters before going for a swim, an almost endless amount of information is available. You could read the writings and explore the classes and programs of people such as Thich Nhat Hanh, Deepak Chopra, Tom Brown Jr., Neale Donald Walsch, Barbara Ann Brennan, the Dalai Lama, Eckhart Tolle, Susan Jeffers, Malcolm Ringwalt, Don Miguel Ruiz, and many more. There is also an increasingly large number of scientists, particularly quantum physicists, who are now supporting the truth that many have known and been living for years. If you are anything like me and don't quite have a grasp of every nuance of quantum physics, a great place to start is with two books, both by Lynne McTaggart (www.lynnemctaggart. com), *The Field* and *The Intention Experiment*. These lay out in easy-to-understand terms what numerous scientists have discovered about our connection to every other life form in the universe and, most importantly, what this means for everyday life.

It is an odd paradox that science as an institution took away the power of personal experience if it could not be measured, tested, or quantified. Now, as we have become more sophisticated in our measuring techniques, we are realizing that the universe and life are far more remarkable than most scientists have believed.

The movement to re-discover the soul and its eternal nature is a tide that will not be turned back; it cannot be stopped. The question is, how many more generations of children will we educate with our current system that is drowning in its own fear? How much longer will we accept educating our children in a manner that is damaging so much life around us?

Below is the first of the *Truly Alive Tips*: physical things you can do for yourself and for the children you share life with that create real, profound change for body, mind and soul. They are designed to support you and your children in creating a space in which you can experience for yourself what is true for you. In this sense they are an invitation to explore further, not a doctrine or prescription. They enable us to cultivate sensitivity to a larger world, and to move increasingly with the flow of life. As we explore we take back control of our own consciousness and we are no longer confined to the prisons we have created for ourselves and, by extension, our children. Don't be put off by the seemingly simplistic nature of the activities. There is real power in them. Many of the world's religions and spiritual cultures teach that we can reach enlightenment or nirvana simply by being aware of breathing in and out. You can't get much simpler than that!

TRULY ALIVE TIP

Bringing The Senses To Life

A remarkably effective way to bring children into the present moment is to encourage them to focus on their senses, bringing them to life. This is one of the first things I teach in my programs to reconnect people with nature, and is both fun and invigorating. Try it now for yourself, allowing time to explore intimately with each sense.

Close your eyes (we are so sight-dominant that, for our other senses to be given a chance, we have to shut our vision down for a few moments). What is the loudest sound you can hear? Listen for a few seconds or a few minutes. Then, focus on the smallest and quietest sound you can hear. Now move to your sense of smell. Breathe in the air through your nose and notice as many different smells as you can. Whenever you do this exercise, you can notice how the air smells in different locations and at different times of day. Next move to your sense of taste, and do the same thing as you did with smell. Taste the air like a lizard! Flick your tongue a few times and then take a big "bite" of it. Again, each time you do this exercise, see if you can taste a difference between locations and times. Next, move on to your sense of touch. Find something that your hands can explore—maybe the bark of a tree, or the morning dew on grass. Let them explore and paint a picture for your mind that is rich and creative. Finally, focus on your sight. As you open your eyes, let them come to rest on something that interests you. Look at it for a few moments as if you have never seen it before. Study the object with absolutely no expectations. Just admire its uniqueness and beauty.

After you have tried these exercises for yourself, walk your children through them. For children, these senses can be given names that speak to their imagination, such as Deer Ears, Raccoon Touch, Coyote Nose, Owl Eyes, and Snake Tongue.

This exploration of the senses can be as short as thirty seconds. Or it can be longer: as long the experience can be concentrated on for, but, more importantly, as long as it can be enjoyed for. It's a great way set the tone at the start of the day, or something to return to in order to regain focus on the present. It's almost impossible to focus on your senses and not be in the present moment. This is a wonderful way to help children be alive.

🌿 🌿 🌿 🌿 🌿 🌿

What I Do for You I Do for Me

Now, let's explore the second part of the statement: We are all made of the same stuff. *That stuff is connected to everything else.* We should understand how this translates to everyday life and, in particular, what it means for educating children.

There are a number of places in the world that illustrate perfectly that we are all connected. Wherever two seas or oceans meet shows us that life is not as black and white as we may think.

I have had the good fortune to see one of these spots: Cape Reinga at the northern tip of New Zealand. It is where you can see quite clearly the Tasman Sea to the west and the Pacific Ocean to the east. As you look one way the Tasman is a very different shade of green-blue to the Pacific. It's palpably obvious they are different oceans, different energies. But where they meet is intriguing. It is a mixing of the two waters, and it is every shade of green and blue imaginable. As your eye travels west you can see the waters become more and more Tasman-like, until you can say with confidence that what you are seeing is purely the Tasman Sea. It is the same the other way. Your eye travels east, along the mixing of the two waters, and gradually the water becomes more Pacific-looking, until at a certain point you can clearly define it as such. But there is no exact point at which you could say that one ocean stops and the other begins. They merge seamlessly into each other, then as they move further away from the center of the mixing pot they assume their own identities. Yet what happens in the Tasman affects the Pacific because they are connected, they share energies, and they literally share life.

If we apply this concept to the whole of creation, it's easy to see that you are connected to me. We are both individuals; we can see where you physically stop and I physically start, but there is a point where our energies meet and mingle, just like the waters. We don't usually see or feel that meeting point as easily as the two oceans (partly because we are out of balance as a result of leaving the soul out of our culture and education, and so we are simply not sensitive enough) but it is where our souls connect. The soul is a larger expression of life. It extends out beyond what we know as our physical body. Just like the oceans in our earlier example there is a point at which we can look at or feel an energy and know exactly what it is. We can say for example, "This is me." But as we move farther out from the center of that energy it begins to dissipate, becoming thinner until, just like the oceans, we are not entirely sure where one energy starts and another stops. In truth these energies never start or stop: it is simply one energy, the everything, the all that is, changing form. We are all one, connected by our souls.

For everyday life, the implications are immense and inspiring. You name it, you are connected to it, and so what we do, positively or negatively, quite literally affects the whole of life.

As we become increasingly conscious of our true, eternal nature, so we will be able to pass this on to our children. Slowly but surely they understand and, most importantly, experience that they are connected to all things. They are able to understand that each being has its own individual consciousness but that their lives are intertwined and deeply connected with all others. They are able to experience that when they give love to another human they are bringing love to themselves; that when they bring peace to everything around them, they also bring peace to themselves; that approaching a simple act, such as eating with joy brings joy to the lives of others around them; and that helping to bring purpose to the life of a friend brings purpose into their own lives.

What we do for others, we do for ourselves. What I do for you I do for me. We not only share life with others, we *are* others, because our souls are one and the same. We just look different, and have a tendency to think that when we can't physically see or touch something, that is where it stops. Yet life exists everywhere, and we are life, so by definition we are everywhere. We are everything. We are life itself, the here, there and everywhere. We are the human and the tree, the animal and the cloud, the river and the star, your brothers and your sisters, even birth and death. We move in all things, and all things move in us, regardless of the degree to which we are conscious of it. We are truly remarkable, and we are most certainly truly alive!

Who Are We?

We could say we work as a teacher, a builder, or a nurse, yet we are not our jobs or our careers. We could say we are American, Indian or Japanese, yet we are not our nationality either. We could say we are black, white, or Hispanic, yet we are not our skin color. We could say we are clever, optimistic, or a critical thinker, yet we are not our thoughts. We could say we are Republican, a Buddhist, or a gay rights activist, yet neither are we our beliefs.

All these are just labels; they are the packaging of our life. They bear no relation to the gift inside, who we really are. We are simply being. And being needs no way of identifying itself, for it just *is*.

The extent of our identification with all our labels in life determines who we think we are, and ultimately whether we will move toward imprisoning or freeing ourselves and our children.

This imprisonment of our children is taking place en mass, in prisons with no walls, no iron bars, no laser beams or door. These prisons have no guns, dogs or anything to stop the inmates coming or going. Yet it remains the most effective, most remarkable prison ever constructed. Its prisoners and guards are one and the same: us. Every time we force children to buy into a label, or think that the packaging is the be all and end all of life, we forget who we really are, and that all we have to do is just *be*.

Our society has become obsessed with the packaging. We even go to war and kill each other if we don't have the right kind of packaging.

Our education systems teach how we can make our packaging bigger, better and shinier. And, if children don't achieve these improvements we perpetuate the myth to them that life as we know it will end. This is one of the things the education system has observed accurately. Life as we know it will indeed end. For when we are able to experience a world beyond labels and packaging, the prisons walls will disappear. We will see clearly for the first time that the freedom we are seeking with such ferocity and violence has been with us all along.

We must teach children that their packaging is beautiful and that we should celebrate every last nuance of our labels. Tall is beautiful, as is short. Chinese is wondrous, as is Tibetan. Muslim is magnificent, as is Christian. But it must be seen for what it really is. The ability to celebrate our packaging and at the same time look upon it with detachment is a true gift. Identification with labels separates; *being*-ness heals. Never looking beyond packaging brings us division; *being*-ness brings us love.

If we could provide children with these experiences their lives would be transformed on all levels: body, mind and soul. We would leave the limited and damaging egocentric world behind, creating instead a larger and grander sense of self. Children would naturally see themselves as part of the magnificent rhythm and dance of life. They would experience that to neglect one part of life is to neglect themselves. Conversely, they would see that to care for all living things is to care for themselves. They would live each moment as if they were the child, the tree, the river, the ocean and the birds. They would feel for themselves that it is the truth. They would see their own life in the lives of others, and the lives of others would be reflected in their own life.

It is almost impossible to have a truly functioning relationship of mutual respect, care and love when there is any kind of hierarchy involved. By refusing to acknowledge that we are all one, we have first separated ourselves from all that is, and then placed ourselves on the top of the pile. Through this sense of superiority, we have been able to justify our actions of destroying the environment, allowing hunger and poverty to continue, and exploiting the less fortunate. Only when we accept that we are no better and no worse than anything or anybody else will we be able to enter into healthy, positive relationships. When we can teach children to look at all forms of life and see themselves within them, we will be providing truly remarkable and loving support. This is why having an educational system with the core belief that we are all one, that we are all connected, is the vital foundation stone to creating lives for children that are full of love, peace, joy, and purpose.

As individuals and as a society, we must find the strength and courage to teach our children *that we are all one*. We can give this gift by choosing to do so.

CHAPTER 4

Why Do We Educate?

The principal goal of education is to create men who are
capable of doing new things, not simply of repeating what
other generations have done.

~Jean Piaget

Snake, Hawk, and Bear

Snake was slithering along on his belly, his tongue flicking in and
out, looking for someone to trick. He was a particularly cruel animal
who seemed to enjoy using his sly words to manipulate and control
others. It didn't take him long to find Hawk, perched high on a cliff,
waiting patiently for the Earth to provide him with a gift of food.
Snake spoke softly through his forked tongue to Hawk: "Aren't you
worried? You work so tirelessly to get food, but you really don't have

any guarantees that all your hard work will pay off? One of these days you might not be so fortunate as you are now, and your luck will run out. I can help you find food easily. Let me see to matters and I'll ensure you'll always have something to eat."

Hawk had never thought about things like that, but the more he considered Snake's words, the more fearful he became and the more he began to doubt himself. Perhaps there was truth in what Snake had said. Could he really take the chance to find out?

Snake saw his opportunity for control and continued. "You must be jealous of Bear, he's very powerful. Look at him, he gets all the food he wants stuffing his big fat belly every minute he gets. He's taking food away from you. If we work together I'll make sure he can't eat all your food." Hawk, heeding Snake's words and envious of Bear's strength, finally relented and agreed to Snake's plan for control.

Snake then turned his attention to Bear and played the same trick, but this time he told Bear about Hawk's incredible ability to spot prey as he flew on the warm winds, saying that Hawk would take all Bear's food if he wasn't careful. He promised that he would keep Hawk tethered to the Earth. Bear, just as envious now of Hawk's flying and hunting as the great bird was of Bear's strength, gave Snake power over him too.

It wasn't long before both Hawk and Bear found themselves in the same boat. Both ended up following Snake's orders, working the fields for him. They became obsessed with just getting enough to get by, scratching out their living. It wasn't long before they forgot their old life and the remarkable gifts the Creator had bestowed upon each of them. In their fear, they had forgotten their true nature.

Both were forgetting entirely whom they had once been they were discovered by a young child with love and joy in her heart. She couldn't understand why they had agreed to such horrible lives. She told them stories of how they once soared with the wind and roamed for miles in the moonlight. She cut the ropes on their wings and feet, and both went back to living in harmony with the Earth. They had no guarantees of crops from Snake, but both Hawk and Bear were free again to enjoy the Creator's gifts of who they really were.

In this story we can see aspects of ourselves in all the animals. The hawk and the bear both represent us when we feel we have to compete against others, instead of having faith in who we are, a beautiful soul, needing nothing. We might feel like we achieve some small victories, as do the animals when they get to grow crops, but these rewards pale into insignificance against the ecstasy that is experienced through embracing our true selves. The snake represents our own worst fears as we talk ourselves into becoming less, absolutely convinced it is the truth. This isn't our fault, it is how we were taught, and society reinforces it on a minute-by-minute basis. But now we are adults we can do something about it, not only for ourselves, but to make sure we do not pass this on to our children.

Desires, Survival, Competing, and Winning

Let's start with the question that underpins so much of our culture: Why do we educate our children?

Education is simply the word we use for guiding the next generation to an understanding of life. Thus, this fundamental question not only decides what form an education system will take but also the direction and nature of the lives of children who experience it. There are really only three reasons we educate today:

- To fulfill the soul's innate desire to learn and experience more.
- To provide independence for our children.
- To ensure we can not only compete, but win.

The first two are very natural desires; the third has been created over centuries and is ingrained in our daily lives to such a degree

that it also appears natural. However, as we shall see, it is a remarkably destructive belief and we would be serving our children well if
we asked deep questions to understand what it creates and why it is
so embedded in our culture. We'll look at each of these reasons for
educating in turn.

The human soul is constantly playing out a cycle of connectedness and seeming separation. When we are here on Earth in our
physical bodies we are seemingly separate from everything else, and
when we do the thing we call "dying" we are seemingly returning
to the Oneness. In reality we are never separate; we are always together as one, and we simply change form, but this is very easy to
forget. So our souls are constantly trying to help us remember the
truth about ourselves and about our relationship with life while we
are here in this world. They are constantly seeking to provide us opportunities that will bring experiences for our body, mind and soul
to know our full and true nature, namely that we are all one—we
always have been and we always will be. The soul's task of providing
these opportunities can be thought of as an in-built, innate desire to
want to explore life to its fullest. We want to learn and experience
all we can, to bring the eternal self into the present, to return home.

We want to feel what it's like to have raindrops hit our cheek,
feel what it's like to be creative, feel what it's like to be at peace and
experience what it's like to inspired. You name it, we want to feel it
for ourselves. If someone else described to us what it felt like to be in
love, would we say, "Okay, that's good enough for me, I don't need to
experience that now"? Of course, this wouldn't cut it in the slightest.
Only when we ourselves feel something does it bring us any kind of
deep satisfaction.

This is the first reason we educate others: to fulfill the soul's
desire to experience life at its grandest and greatest. We yearn for
this for both ourselves and for our children. The soul is the little
voice inside us urging us to climb mountains, find cures for ill-

nesses, learn a musical instrument or sit in meditation. The desire on the part of the soul is not to master the "doing" aspect of these activities but to revel in what we are *being* when we are doing them.

The second reason we educate is arguably the simplest: to ensure the next generation is independent, and can take care of its own needs. We show children how to feed and clothe themselves and how to perform life's basic tasks, so that one day they can live without us.

The last reason we educate is to teach children how to outcompete life to ensure their survival. This is the belief we desperately need to address because it is highly destructive, causing much suffering to many forms of life, not just our own. It is so damaging because it is a direct product of one of our most harmful emotions: fear.

A recent news report on the television highlights a fairly typical way this is played out. Economists were extremely worried at the lack of progress by teenagers in educational tests. They said America might not be able to compete in the near future. This is perpetuated at every level of society, and nowhere more fervently than the education system, for it relies on people buying into this fallacy to justify its own existence. If we did not have to compete, why on earth would we choose this damaging system? We simply would not. It would be seen as completely untenable, ridiculous even. So the alleged grave consequences of being unable to outcompete others is constantly repeated as if it should consume our every thought—which of course it does. Because it consumes our every thought, we have adopted it as one of the most fundamental truths that exists. It is one of our most basic cultural myths, running through every facet of society, even our religions. We must look deeply into this "truth," and not accept others' ideas as our own, for it may be this belief, so ingrained, that sees our society crumble under the weight of its own illusions.

Let's take a closer look at where this idea stems from. We believe we must be able to compete or, more accurately, win at this game called life in order to survive. Surviving means getting the finite resources we need any way we can. So in order to decide who gets what they "need" we create winners and losers and, so long as we are part of the winners' group, we can not only forget about the losers, but also justify our actions because it's "survival of the fittest." This is a term that has been pounced upon by people to mean that the winners are right, period. We say that if one thing dominates another (outcompetes it), it is stronger and fitter, and if it is fitter it must have earned the right to survive, regardless of how it does so. Therefore we justify our actions against each other and against other forms of life because in our minds we humans are the strongest, the most superior. But are we really the fittest if our own survival depends on the destruction of most other forms of life? In the long run we are actually bringing about our own downfall, raising the question, who is really winning when we outcompete others? Do you win a race to the top of a tree if the only way you can do so is to cut the tree down as you climb? Of equally faulty logic in the case of human versus human is the misguided belief that one section of the population can win against or is superior to another. Depending on the fight it could be for example black, white, American, Japanese, female, male, young, old, rich, poor, educated, uneducated, Jewish or Muslim. Yet one soul can never be superior to any other. A drop of water in the Pacific Ocean is not superior to one in the Atlantic. We are not superior to the things we currently dominate, or inferior to the things we may be dominated by. The idea of 'survival of the fittest', so prevalent in our world, is based on a number of faulty assumptions, none of which are serving us or our children in experiencing lives that are full of love, peace, joy, or purpose.

The first of these assumptions is that we won't survive. Yet the soul cannot die or perish. It is life itself and will always be so, now and forever. Everything that is, the *all* of life, cannot suddenly become less than everything. And everything that is cannot all of a sudden give birth to something brand new, something outside of itself. Therefore, we will always *be*, though the form we take may change. The complete identification with only a physical body and life therefore forces us to shrink toward a much smaller world, where survival is not only not guaranteed, but is, in the long term, impossible. Our current experience is that sooner or later everything "dies". Everything has its time, and then it is no more. We see death as failure, a travesty even, instead of simply part of the flow and rhythms of life. We are that rhythm, we are that flow, and so we will always *be*. The move towards a less overwhelming, fearful and damaging experience for our children begins with adults exploring and hopefully expanding their notion of self toward one that is far grander and more accurately represents who we are.

The second assumption is that there is not enough. By its very definition, the Oneness—all that is—is enough! It can't possibly lack anything, because it is everything. Everything that is can't need anything outside itself, because there is nothing outside it. If we can never "die", what can we possibly need? We can need something to maintain a certain form, that is to say, to keep our packaging (body, thought, beliefs etc) working, but the part of us that is without form, our eternal being, can need nothing. Life provides for itself to live in balance, and we are part of that give and take, the to and fro of energy, the circles and the cycles.

Even without these non-physical definitions, there is more than enough food to feed us all. It's just that some parts of the world throw away enough food each day to feed those who are starving. There is plenty of money to go around. It's just that some people in the world hoard obscene amounts of wealth while millions of others cannot afford clean drinking water. Most societies don't need to use the Earth's resources at even a fraction of the level they do right now, but we refuse to change our beliefs and actions because we are afraid someone else will grab what we have, so that they will be the fittest, surviving at our expense. Furthermore, by taking far more than we need, against the laws of nature, we are effectively declaring we are more important than our children and grandchildren. We are literally taking today the resources they will need tomorrow. We will not give up our luxuries that we have fought so hard to win. Yet there is no luxury and no reward in constantly having to stay at the top of the pile, with fear snapping at our heels like a pack of wild dogs—especially if you can only stay at the top by exploiting and damaging others. True luxury is found when we realize we can let go of our fears, fall back into the arms of the Oneness and find there is enough, for everybody and everything. We have always been life itself and we will always continue to do be.

Yes, we have to take from the world. Each day we have to consume food and water of some kind, otherwise our bodies will not sustain themselves. Yet we do not need to fear this eventuality. If we do not sustain ourselves we will simply become a gift to other life forms, just as other life forms have been a gift to us every day of our lives. We also have choice about *how* we take. We can consume as if it is our god-given right because we view ourselves as the most superior beings on the planet, or we can see ourselves as part of the natural ebb and flow of life, only taking what we need because we realize and understand that life is precious.

The flow and rhythm of life, that we have attempted to remove ourselves from, help us to remember all that we need to know. A deer eats green grass, and when the deer dies its body replenishes the grass, helping it to grow tall and proud. The deer and grass are not competing against each other, they are part of the same cycle. That cycle extends to the whole web of life, humans included. If the deer were to eat all the grass in one area they would either starve, or move to a different place to feed. If they continue to take all the grass from everywhere they can reach, there will be no more grass and the deer will surely experience what we know as death. The deer needs the grass, just as the grass needs the deer. Our physical needs are similar.

We require clean air, clean water and healthy food to live in our bodies. We therefore have a need *not* to outcompete that with which we have a mutually beneficial relationship: the whole of life.

Fear

When we live in constant fear, with no apparent hope of its ever ending, our experience of life is hugely diminished. It negatively affects every single aspect of our being from physical and mental health to creativity and potential. It may well be that one day scientists prove fear to be one of the most destructive forces on the planet. Whenever we feel fear creeping into our lives, or into our education systems, we must explore every nuance of it and find out where our breakdown in understanding is. Almost always it is because we perceive ourselves as separate from each other and from the rest of life.

Author of the *Conversations with God* series, Neale Donald Walsch, has a particularly appropriate acronym for fear: Fantasy Expressed As Reality. We often believe with every ounce of our being that we should fear something, when in fact this is simply not true; it is fantasy which we have created, either on our own, or—usually—as a result of learning it from others. When I look at my own life, I can see clearly that this has been evident on a daily basis. I felt fearful of leaving my successful career and following my heart because I reasoned I would run out of money and would not survive. But I overcame my fear and, though I now certainly have less money, I am not only surviving, in terms of my soul and a balance in life, I'm actually thriving. Every day, I constantly question what I believe and what I have learned in order to discern fantasy from reality and move to a place where my unfounded fear does not overwhelm me.

It can take great courage to look at something we fear and release ourselves from its paralyzing effects. If we are to create a more loving, peaceful world for children, we have to build a new foundation of beliefs that more accurately represent reality, and not our own unrealistic fears. Without this, real and lasting change will not be possible. With a grander belief of who we are, we can leave fear behind. This is only possible if we can lead our children not just to obtain conceptual understandings but to have real, hands-on experiences of the interconnectedness of the whole of life . This is the key to the treasures of life. It is the doorway to a heaven on Earth. This is the world we must nurture and immerse ourselves in, any way we possibly can. Only then the storm clouds can part, and we can remember that we are in paradise again—where we have always been.

The Core of Your Truth

The ability to take every belief we have formed and, one by one, slowly but surely hold them up to the scrutiny of truth is one of the greatest tools we have to create a new world. Do the beliefs we currently hold reflect our true nature? Do they lead us and our children to Oneness and to pure being? Do they promote love, peace, joy, and purpose in our life experience? If they do not, it is time to change them, as simply as you would change your shirt if it were the wrong color. The challenge is that we can become very emotionally attached to our beliefs, and this emotion clouds our ability to think rationally, and it certainly clouds our ability to feel what life is actually telling us. How to move past this emotional barrier? Acknowledge that it exists. Accept that it is there, and that while there are areas in our lives where our emotions serve us remarkably well, this is not one of them. When we accept a truth, we own it, and when we own it, change no longer has to induce fear in us and cause us to respond irrationally through our emotions.

Many strange ideas have arisen around the desire to question our beliefs. In particular, accusations of being unpatriotic, unholy, immoral, and even just downright stupid are labels that are often thrown at those who seek any kind of change. Yet there is nothing unpatriotic, unholy or immoral and certainly nothing stupid in asking, *why?* in a loving, peaceful manner. Do the people who throw these accusations at others have a vested interest in their being a certain way and doing certain things? Are they using these accusations to maintain a world of competition and fighting because they consider themselves to be in the winners' group?

If we do not put aside our emotional attachments and begin critically examine our deepest held beliefs, we will slip further and further into the world of darkness, fear and oppression that we are already creating. Nobody wins in this world so steeped in separation and negativity. We are not on the cusp of this world, we are already in it, entrenched. Whenever we feel compelled to turn away from a part of life because it causes us pain to look at, we should continue the examination and exploration of our beliefs to find out how our lives came to be created and experienced the way they did. Can we look at the homeless on the street, the starving children of the world, the slaughter, genocide and murder of fellow humans, the inexplicable cruelty to nature, the greed of our society, the fear in people's eyes, the oppression of entire nations and the exploitation of every form of life that is taking place just to serve our "needs"? This is what the belief in needing to outcompete life has created. It is incredibly destructive, and yet deeply pervasive. If we cannot look at these without them causing us pain, it is most obviously time to change.

If these horrific, needless creations are also what you see, I encourage you to ask the simple question, why do we educate? Peel down through every layer as far as you can to the very core of your truth. Does it contain a need to educate children in violence and competition, or does it contain a desire to educate children in love, and in freedom?

Could There Be Something More?

What if it is possible we don't know everything, that our understandings of exactly how life works are incomplete? What if we don't have all the information? Admitting we don't know something goes against one of the most ingrained behaviors in our society. Our culture tells us to be strong, to not show any kind of weakness. (Because that might result in our leaving the winners' group.) We are taught that when we meet someone for the first time, we should shake their hand very firmly, look them in the eye, and let them see and feel just how strong we are. We continue to vote for politicians, even if we know they are lying through their teeth, but not if they admit they just got something wrong. The ultimate weakness it seems in our society is to show any sign that we might not have all the answers. Yet if we are to serve our children, the first thing we should do is look around, with humility, and acknowledge that given the way we live we obviously do not know everything.

There was a remarkable study, conducted by Harvard Medical School in the 1970's that involved two sets of kittens. Both sets were of course fed, watered, and cared for. One group was placed in a room that had nothing but vertical black and white stripes on all the walls. The second group was placed in a room that again had nothing but black and white stripes on the walls, but these ones were horizontal. When the two groups of kittens were brought together into a "normal" room the most remarkable things happened. Those kittens who has been brought up in the vertically striped room would happily walk round the uprights of chair legs, but could not perceive the cross beams, the horizontal pieces of the chairs. They would repeatedly walk straight into those. The exact opposite occurred with the kittens who had only known the horizontal striped room. They would avoid the horizontal cross-pieces of the chairs, but would walk straight into the vertical uprights as if they did not exist. Quite evidently, the rooms they had grown up in allowed them to perceive only certain parts of reality. The implications for our lives are huge. There could be different worlds going on right now in front of our eyes, or different aspects of life we are unable to acknowledge, but because our brains are so used to a certain world, just like those kittens, we may not actually be able to detect them with our senses. It suggests that our understanding of reality is almost certainly not complete and that there is so much more out there, just waiting to be discovered.

Not knowing everything is not the challenge we must address. We can't ever possibly know it all. Rather, the challenge before us is to stop pretending and convincing ourselves that we have all the information. We can feel deflated by this, or we can feel elated. We can feel inspired because we understand there is always more to discover, and that everything we think we know could be changed in an instant. Clinging to our current way of life could be scary because someone could pull the rug from under our feet at a moments notice. But if we are already seeking change, if we feel in our hearts that there is still more that life has to offer us, and more that we have to offer life, then the admission that we don't know everything is remarkably empowering. We don't have to waste any more energy on thumping our chest like a gorilla, or crowing like a rooster to appear all knowing and all powerful. The energy we save from those false pretences can be put toward what is actually important: creating a world in which children can be truly alive. Will we be making it up as we go along? Absolutely. Will we get every single step correct? Not a chance! Can we really create that new world? In a heartbeat, yes. Humility is not simply a way of honoring other people, it is a way of honoring life itself.

TRULY ALIVE TIP 🍃🍃🍃🍃🍃🍃

Gratitude

Simply saying "thank you" is a wonderful way to help children connect with the world around them. There are always an infinite number of things we can be grateful for. As we encourage children to say thank you, they will be reminded that life is giving them an abundance of gifts, bringing them everything they truly need. If you are grateful for something, you are making a statement about your awareness of it in your life.

We should support children in giving thanks in a way that feels right for them. It could be verbally—out loud—or silently in their minds. It could be by dancing or painting or working out a mathematics problem. We can be grateful in all that we do and all that we are. Children are not just going to do this by themselves—they need a genuine example from the adults around them. A good way to begin making this part of a child's life is to find something to say thank you for before each meal you share together. Depending on the number of people, maybe one person can lead everyone else, or perhaps there is time and space for each person to have a voice and to be heard. The words that we say are relatively unimportant. It is the feeling behind them that carries the creative power. If all that happens before a meal is that somebody simply repeats what has been said for the last three years without passion or sincerity, the act is largely wasted. Only give thanks when you really mean it, and demonstrate to children with your own actions that the feeling is more important than the words.

🌿 🌿 🌿 🌿 🌿 🌿

Free and Full Expression of Life

If we wish for our children to be able to leave fear behind we must completely discard our basic belief in teaching them so they may outcompete everyone and everything else. It does not serve the lives of children in positive ways. The belief that will replace it is so simple that I am sure many people will dismiss it. Nevertheless, it is the belief that will leave no other path to walk than the path to unconditional love, total peace, complete joy, and deep purpose. Life, and the soul are, after all, the essence of simplicity.

As individuals and as a society, we must find the strength and courage to give children the gift of honoring the belief that *education exists simply to ensure the free and full expression of the individual*. We can give this gift by choosing to do so.

What does this mean? It means that each child will be *free* to make choices that are based in love, not surrounded by fear. This is the birthright of every human being. It means that education exists for children to fully explore who they are, and what their relationships are to life. We really do not know what it means to be fully human because the potential of life is so great we may never reach the limit. But the adventure and possibility of discovery must be open to us, and we must demonstrate to children that the experience can be enjoyed. If we put limits on what children can fully explore, we are putting limits on life. These limits are set for us as children just as the kittens in the striped room had their limits set for them. If we think that our current version of reality is the only place that life exists then inevitably we will create invisible barriers. Our children will reach them, stop, and become stagnant and frustrated because they are unable to experience the world beyond them, the one thing our souls are yearning to do.

By its very definition, life, or our soul, cannot be contained nor have limits placed upon it. We do not know where it begins and ends. It is endless, without edges or sides. Life has even been called the great unknown because we will never reach a point at which we understand every single part of it. Therefore, we should give our children the gift of life and an education that is as free and as full as our understanding can make it.

I have had the pleasure of working with a number of families over extended periods, sharing with them how to reconnect with nature.

Some of these families have adopted the belief of freedom and fullness of expression and given this gift to their children from the moment they were born. These youngsters grow up very differently from many of their peers in mainstream education. To some, the children who have been granted more freedom may seem unruly, ask too many questions, or have a little too much independence. To me, they have amazingly creative, inquisitive minds, and most importantly, they have retained a love for learning when others have left it behind. The gift creates a kind of freedom that children seem to revel in. I always look forward to working with these youngsters because they have a zest and a passion to discover life. Even though these children have been granted more freedom, the family unit has not broken down but actually grown tighter, and learning has not taken a back seat to video games. In fact the opposite is true. Our fears can prevent us from giving a gift as powerful as this, but it doesn't have to be this way. We each have the capacity to give this gift of free and full expression of life.

If we return to the two natural reasons we educate (to fulfill our soul's desire to experience life to the full and to create independence in children) and leave out the third (outcompete everybody and everything) we will take the dreams we hold in our hearts and make them a reality. We will learn what it is to love and to share because we will desire it from the very core of our being. Poverty will leave us. We will experience deep, lasting peace because we will no longer have to fight. Wars will be the stories we tell our grandchildren about when we forgot there was enough, and we didn't have to compete. We will experience what it is to be completely filled with joy because we will know that we are very safe and very secure. Depression will be yesterday's news. And, we will experience what it is to have a purpose beyond our self because we can only truly serve ourselves when we serve and honor the whole of life.

The role of the new education system will, in a sense, mimic the role of life itself. It will give the individual the opportunity to fully explore and experience themselves and the world around them. In doing so, it will hand each soul the ultimate freedom—the knowledge that they are indeed free to express themselves in any way they choose. We will not ask anything of our children, just as life asks nothing from us. You could say that we are going back to basics. Not basic in the sense of what it means in terms of education, but what it means in terms of life. This will strip away all the baggage that our society has collected and get right to the heart of the matter. From our hearts, we can give the gift of a free and full education as a means of ensuring the free and full expression of the individual child.

CHAPTER 5

Celebrating Uniqueness

Today you are You, that is truer than true.

There is no one alive who is Youer than You.

~Dr. Seuss

Uniqueness

What do all children have in common? For a start, they are all quite remarkable. All children are special and contribute to the remarkable world we live in. Every child wants to discover, to have adventures, to play, and to experience this amazing thing called being alive. They all like to be happy, healthy, and free—just the same as adults. Children are all identical in these aspects. And that's where their similarities begin and end.

69

Beyond this, children are as different as snowflakes on a wintry day or grains of sand on the beach. No two are ever the same. They all have different passions, different desires, and different ways of experiencing life. Each one is unique.

I want to share with you an experience that helped me to realize that, as a society, we don't actually understand this concept of uniqueness. Or, if we do understand, we don't care enough to find the willpower to honor it. We have decided that it is not only round pegs we are trying to force into square holes, it is every conceivable shape in the universe. The story I am about to tell is important not because it is remarkable—on the contrary, it is decidedly ordinary, and its very ordinariness is why it is so crucial for us to hear.

John's Story

In my earliest years as an elementary school teacher, I had a class of around thirty children—an average-sized class. I had been teaching no more than six months, when an incident occurred that has stayed with me in a profound way ever since. A boy in the class called John, about seven years old, took every opportunity to misbehave. This didn't especially perturb me; there are usually a number of similar children in a classroom, and it is fair to say their misbehavior mostly stems from boredom.

John, being one of those "difficult" children, was only just tolerated in the classroom. The teachers tried to make sure he had things to keep him occupied, but not too much was expected of him. As long as his misbehavior didn't spread too far across the classroom, the day was considered successful. John found it frustrating to have to read and write. He could do it, but he avoided it if at all possible.

This particular day started with English as it normally did, and John was his usual self. He was not working. He was predictably distracted and was also distracting others. I had to spend a lot of time and energy trying to prevent him from disrupting the entire classroom, let alone get any productive work out of him. As usual, it was a battle between him trying to escape a world he did not want to be in, and me, representing the system he was rebelling against, trying to drag him back into that reality because that was what was expected.

The first lesson finished, and we were changing over to the next—woodwork. We were going to make picture frames that the children had each designed a week before. In my mind, I winced. If I were honest with myself, I was dreading letting John anywhere near the scissors, glue, wood, glitter, and other items that I was sure he could think of a thousand inappropriate uses for.

The lesson began and I quickly became busily occupied with helping all the children with their projects. A long time passed, perhaps half an hour or more, when I suddenly had a terrible feeling. I realized I had not heard a thing from John. Why hadn't I kept an eye on him? This could be bad. I quickly scanned the room for John, looking at all the usual places where he wasn't supposed to be.

Finally I spotted him, sitting at his desk silently, apparently disengaged from the rest of the class. Hesitantly, I approached him, and he showed me—to my surprise—an extraordinarily beautiful picture frame. Then he picked up another one and said he was already on his second. They were probably as good as someone twice his age could have done in the same amount of time. I told him they were outstanding, gave him as much praise as I could, and left him to it; I didn't want to disturb him any further. By the time the class was finished, he had made three picture frames in the time almost all the other children had struggled to make one. Each one was made with care and precision and decorated beautifully.

I was astounded and speechless. I think back to it now and it brings tears to my eyes. Right there, for that one hour, John had come alive. His eyes were happy and dancing for the first time. He indeed had skills, passions, and interests; he just almost never got the opportunities to experience them. In that brief time in the classroom, John was freely and fully expressing himself, something he almost never got the opportunity to do. It was a real awakening for me as a teacher.

Every child wants to experience being truly alive, but we can't expect that one path will provide the opportunities for them all to do so. Given the chance, even the "worst" children, the most badly behaved, the most destructive, the most bored and even the most apathetic, can and do regain a sparkle in their eye and a love for life, but only if we allow their uniqueness to be celebrated, not deflated and cast aside.

TRULY ALIVE TIP

Let's Pretend

Developing a child's imagination is important for a number of reasons. It helps children to be creative in many aspects of their lives. I have found that those children with strong imaginations are usually more independent than those who struggle to visualize in their minds. Imaginative children can adapt to change more easily because change happens frequently in their minds. A healthy fluidity develops where life does not have to show up a certain way for children to be truly alive. Finally, and possibly most importantly, when children can imagine themselves as doing or being other things, a strong connection develops with those things they are imagining. For example, children who play at being animals usually have a strong emotional bond with them. These connections in the mind bring about an increased sense of connection to life. We should therefore encourage children to use their imaginations in as many different ways as possible.

A positive experience for children is to pretend they are another part of life: an animal, a tree, or even the rain, for example. We can support children in this kind of play by encouraging them to fully imitate the thing they are pretending to be. Movement, behaviors, and even thoughts can all be added to the play. So, instead of just growling like a mountain lion, they can move like a mountain lion, see and hear and taste like mountain lion, and even think like a mountain lion. This allows children to perceive the world from a much richer perspective, and helps them to honor and make deep connections with different forms of life.

Why Is Honoring Uniqueness so Difficult for Us?

There are two reasons why we currently find it difficult to honor the gift of uniqueness. First, there is the question of economics. If we try to honor that every child is unique within the confines of the current educational model, we would almost certainly need more teachers. And this of course could only happen at great expense. For many years, government budgets for public school education have shown that we do not want to radically change the education system in this way. So, the focus of teaching remains away from honoring the individual and more toward fulfilling the "needs" of society. (Get a job and contribute financially to at least 3 percent growth per year, ensuring our nation are the winners.)

The second reason why we find it difficult to honor the uniqueness of every child is that we as adults have decided that we know what is best for children. Despite perceiving (wrongly) that life is to be feared, we have survived thus far. We claim to understand what it takes to survive, and we naturally want the next generation to do the same. To that end, we have formed committees and curricula and decided in advance exactly (and I do mean *exactly*) what children will be taught, and thus what they will experience. While on the surface this may seem very noble and in the best interests of every child, we have in fact done this in the best interests of ourselves. If we observe objectively, we can see clearly that most adults in society want children to grow up either to maintain the status quo or to continue going in the same direction the adults themselves chose, mainly because we as adults are fearful of change. (Right now, most of the people who read this book are in the "winners' group". So we see little reason to change and risk being "losers," even though it should be painfully obvious that when one person loses, we all lose.)

If we truly honored children as individuals, we would help them to understand that their life is indeed *their* life, and that we make no judgment as to which direction or experiences in life they choose. It is not that we do not care, it is because we understand who we really are—that we are eternal souls, incapable of being harmed or damaged in any way—that we are able to let go of the need to control. We are able to grant children true freedom because we understand the truth: that every choice we make for ourselves is perfect for us to re-claim our birthright of being truly alive. Nothing happens to us that is outside the Oneness, and therefore every path is the path back to love and freedom, for this is all that exists. For example, it is not right to tell a child that they will find more success (read: be more likely to survive in the constant competition against life) by becoming a celebrated brain surgeon as opposed to, say, a street cleaner. We make these judgments because we perceive one as being higher up the ladder of life than the other, and we completely disregard the joy and sense of purpose the "lowlier" career may bring to an individual.

In a world of honoring uniqueness, we can no longer deal in hierarchies. Hierarchies separate us from life, turning relationships of mutual respect and love into ones of domination and subordination, righteousness and fear. Is a ten-year-old superior to a three-year-old? Is a bumblebee better than a ladybug? I imagine you can hear the absurdity in those questions. But ask if the ten-year-old is superior to the bumblebee, and that might elicit some agreement. We must look deeply into the hierarchies we hold, for we all have them, and they are all illusions. We have made them all up. By beginning to allow them to change from "superior" to simply "different," we will start to dismantle our judgments about these hierarchies, opening the door for a true relationship of mutual respect and honor to flourish. In the story that opened this chapter, it would be easy to think that John was an "inferior" child because he found it frustrating to read and write. But these were not his passions, not who he really was. We wouldn't criticize a bumblebee for not being the size of an elephant. Yet it would be equally wrong to say that, when allowed to undertake something that spoke to his heart, John suddenly became superior. He is what he and every child and each part of life always are: unique.

When we stop honoring the gift of uniqueness, we stop honoring life itself. Every single part of the universe is unique. As we honor this quality in every child, we take huge steps toward providing a life experience for them that is full of love, peace, joy, and purpose.

As individuals and as a society, we must find the strength and courage to give children the gift of honoring their own gifts, of honoring the fact that *every child is unique*. We can give this gift by choosing to do so.

CHAPTER 6

Rethinking Success

An educational system isn't worth a great deal
if it teaches young people how to make a living but
doesn't teach them how to make a life.

~author unknown

Sarah's Passion

I have observed numerous people while they are teaching children. I have seen different adults teach the same thing to almost identical groups, in identical settings, yet the differences in what children took from the experience were vast. Two people spring to mind who worked with me at a nature-based school. The first, Rob, had a wealth of knowledge about plants. He could tell you almost anything about them, from their growing habits, to pollination strategies, and even if they were edible. When he took children off to learn about plants, they would return very knowledgeable. They could relate some interesting facts and had obviously paid attention to what Rob said. He was certainly a good teacher.

Another teacher I saw in action, Sarah, possessed something that is more valuable than gold: passion. At first, I was reluctant to let her lead a group, because she didn't know as much as Rob. But whenever she talked about plants, there was a spark in her eyes that no amount of studying can bring. She loved plants, not from simply a collection of facts and knowledge, but as something that had a profound impact on her life. We could all easily see that she could feel her connection to plants on a deep level. She seemed to understand their souls, and saw them as friends and equals.

When the children came back from Sarah's first time leading the group, they plunged straight into plant books and began asking her dozens more questions. Most importantly, though, there was an aliveness in the children's eyes that told of the magical world Sarah had delivered to them. They had actually taken on some of Sarah's passion. She had opened the door to wonderful experiences with plants for those children, not through information, but by allowing them to share in her love for them.

Love and Passion

Love and passion should absolutely be central to educating children. We need to start laying the foundations for children to become *lifelong learners* and *lovers of life*. You certainly can't be these without passion.

The twin ideals of love and passion are almost interchangeable in an educational context. For example, we could say our greatest passion is chemistry, or that we love it. We understand from both words that chemistry is what excites us and we want to learn all we can about it. If we want to be more accurate, we could say that passion brings about love. Humans usually develop love for something they are passionate about, which is vitally important for the role of the teacher, as we will see shortly.

One of the biggest questions in education is, how do we achieve success? In this context, do love and passion lead to success? An answer we would do well to explore is that love and passion *are* success. They do not lead to anything; they are success in and of themselves. It would be like asking, how do we become human? Of course, the question is quite meaningless. We are already human; it is not a goal we have to reach. We are successful at being human when we are alive, just as we are successful at learning when we are being loving and passionate. As we begin to change from *doing* to *being*, we will discover that we would do well to encourage children to do nothing that is simply a means to an end. The experience along the way should be the real focus of our desire for "success."

When a child asks me about the natural world, this stems from a desire to know more, to discover its secrets. I have to tell myself that it may be the only question the child will ever ask about the Earth. What they ask and the answer I give are not the most important part of the interaction. The *way* I answer is. I want them to see in my eyes, my voice and my soul that the secrets of nature are worth working hard for and that they bring every aspect of our being to life. I want the child to understand, by looking at my example, how much joy it can bring to them. I'm not really too concerned in a short interaction as to whether they remember what I say or not. I don't want them to learn only for a few minutes, I want them to be able to learn for the rest of their life, and that is only possible if the child creates an internal deep-rooted desire to discover more.

What will the next child that asks you about your passion receive? Will they merely receive information, or will they look in your eyes and see that your passion has brought you to an ecstatic relationship with life? Will they remember a simple fact or will they feel the answer in their very soul? Will they learn for a few moments, or will they learn for a lifetime?

Where Does Love Come From?

Think about love for a moment. (It's a good thing to think about!) Perhaps to you it's something immensely complex. Perhaps it's something wonderfully simple. Possibly it's both. Think of something or someone you love. Now ask yourself this question: Why do you love that certain thing or that certain someone? Go ahead and make a list of every single reason in the world that you can think of. It is almost certain that your list does not include either of the following:

• Someone else told me I should feel that way.

• There is a law that says I should.

Love cannot and will never come from an external source. It cannot be ordered or legislated. Love comes from the individual. The individual is love, and love is the individual. It is our very essence—our very being. Yet this can be forgotten; it can fall by the wayside.

Experience is the most powerful tool we have in this. It is the role of the teacher to lead children toward experiencing love. Love for themselves, for others, and for the world around them. With this teaching, as children mature, they will realize that they themselves are the source for the love of life that they feel.

It is fair to say that it is more beneficial for a child to receive an education from a teacher who is bursting with passion but slightly lacking in knowledge than one who knows a great deal but lacks passion. This is because passion breeds passion. It's wonderfully infectious and inspiring. I believe that you don't so much see passion in others as feel it; much of it is intangible. As soon as we move into feelings, the doorway is opened to the soul and to a larger, deeper, more fulfilling experience. If we can only pass this on to children, they will, under their own impetus, gain far more knowledge and certainly more wisdom in their own lives than we as teachers could ever share with them.

It is very clear that humans, regardless of age, are successful in what they are passionate about. They become knowledgeable, capable, and usually highly informed about those aspects of life that they *love*. It doesn't matter if it's being a car mechanic, a relationship counselor, or a farmer. Passion and love equals success. Using our current limited definition of success as leading to something—making a good living, ensuring job security, or contributing to the economy—it ticks all the right boxes. But far more important is that the definition of success includes—and prioritizes—the *free* and *full* expression of the individual: an expression of the soul. Why? Because the *soul* is happy. The *soul* is joyful. That part of us that is so often forgotten gets a chance to come and play. A child who is passionate is truly alive!

Balancing Knowledge and Wisdom

Knowledge can be defined as "acquaintance with facts, truths, or principles, as from study or investigation" (www.dictionary.reference. com). Wisdom can be defined as "the quality of being wise; knowledge *and the capacity to make use of it*" (my emphasis) (www.dictionary. net).

These definitions are important to note in order to redress an imbalance that is causing us all considerable pain. We have become a society that worships knowledge (particularly technological) and have forgotten that, without the wisdom to use it, it is largely wasted. Worse still, in many cases knowledge without wisdom can be downright dangerous. For example, our knowledge has given us the ability to set up platforms above the ocean. From these we drill down miles into the seabed and somehow manage to collect oil from the earth beneath the sea. That takes a tremendous amount of knowledge.

Unfortunately, we do not have the wisdom to realize that when things go wrong with the extraction process we may not have the ability to cope, and the result of a major spill is enormously damaging for all life forms concerned. The damage caused throws both the environment and the economy off balance, and the whole world suffers as a result. (Of course the next layer down, the question of our reliance on this source of energy at all could and should highlight our profound lack of wisdom.)

Another example: in early 2011, the earthquake in Japan where the Fukushima nuclear plant teetered on the brink of complete meltdown should have shown us we do not currently have the wisdom to make use of the knowledge we have. This has not necessarily always been life threatening, but recently two things have changed that have highlighted (or should have highlighted) the fragility of things. First, technology has progressed to the stage that if we do not use it wisely we will destroy ourselves. Second, our world population has expanded to such a degree that we are placing unprecedented pressures on the environment. We no longer have room for error, but with our current lack of wisdom the outcome for many forms of life looks increasingly bleak.

Imagine a child being given the knowledge of how to work a gun, but never being given the wisdom of how to use it. It would be a disaster waiting to happen. In fact, in many tragic cases, it already has happened. We must bring gaining both knowledge and wisdom back into balance for the sake of all living things.

Hands-on Experience

When teaching children, there are two key factors to consider in order to develop and then maintain a balance between the knowledge gained and the wisdom to use it properly.

Firstly, wherever and whenever possible, knowledge should be acquired through direct, hands-on experience. For example, if a girl is passionate about ecology, it would be beneficial for her to gain knowledge by actively participating in the habitat she is studying, and by personally experiencing the different relationships within the ecosystem. After even a short time, she would understand the intricacies and nuances of life on a far deeper level than all the books and websites in the world could convey adequately. Instead of learning certain things in isolation, she would discover how everything is connected and interrelated. From these hands-on experiences, she would gain the precious insight that we are all one. As John Muir put it, "When one tugs at a single thing in nature, he finds it attached to the rest of the world." Hands-on experience goes a long way in developing a balance between knowledge and wisdom in almost any field you can think of. Even business studies could be transformed. Children could study an aspect of a working business and understand that it does not stand in isolation from the rest of that organization nor, indeed, from the rest of the world.

Informational texts should be used to enhance rather than form the backbone of knowledge acquisition. They are limited in their ability to teach anything more than a skeleton framework of understanding. One problem of only teaching knowledge in this manner is that as children grow older and pass more tests they see themselves as becoming very clever. Their own sense of cleverness is reinforced in the adult world because they are rewarded for their knowledge acquisition in terms of modern-day success. But although it may appear to be so, their knowledge is not nearly complete; the wisdom of experiencing that all things are connected is almost always missing.

As adults, we try to solve problems in isolation, using knowledge that we consider to be very powerful, when in reality the problems are far more complex and interconnected than our learning has allowed us to comprehend. Thinking of problems as being isolated from each other shows we do not understand the depth of the interconnectedness that surrounds us. We come up with isolated solutions that profit either one species (humans) or one section of the species (white, black, Asian, American, male, female, Christians, Muslims, etc.). Then we scratch our heads and wonder why so many people are unhappy, unhealthy, or dying. Teaching mere knowledge does not allow us to penetrate beneath the surface of our understanding of life. It leads our answers to life's problems to be similarly short-sighted. Supporting children to develop wisdom in balance with their knowledge allows them personally to experience that we are all one. Their solutions to life's problems become richer and more far reaching because they understand that what they do for others they do for themselves. So wisdom also creates opportunities for a deep purpose beyond the self to develop.

When we place knowledge over personal experience, another less obvious problem for children is that their view of the world can quickly be narrowed instead of expanded. In the way we currently teach, everything in the world receives a label, for example, a *forest*, a *painting*, an *old woman* or a *robin*. What happens is that children think they know something because they know the label, when in fact they really know and have experienced very little. Content with knowing the label, they have little desire to go and discover more. Why would they want to learn more? As a society, we reward label collectors, those who have a great store of knowledge, by defining this as success. Schools reinforce it by creating environments that on the whole do not encourage personal experience and exploration. And— illustrating the level of obsession we have with labels—too often we teach that it is more important to be able to spell the label correctly than it is actually to have an experience with the thing itself. It doesn't matter how you spell happiness if you don't *experience* it.

Before leaving my job as an elementary school teacher, I considered myself quite clever—at least above average. I knew quite a lot of facts, certainly enough to answer most questions that children had, and certainly enough to be successful in this culture. Then I met Tom Brown Jr., who told me a story of what his mentor, an Apache elder named Stalking Wolf (or Grandfather, as he was affectionately known), had shown him about robins when he was a child. It changed my whole outlook on what it means to learn.

Robins and Pine Trees

Grandfather crouched on a small trail in the Pine Barrens of New Jersey, staring intently into the bushes. Tom, being a child and wanting to learn as much as he could from his remarkable friend, stared down the trail too, emulating Grandfather's stillness. Tom thought that whatever was in the bushes must be something really worth seeing. He crept as slowly as he could toward Grandfather, not wishing to scare what he assumed must be a rare and special animal in the bushes, just out of sight. When he reached his mentor, Grandfather was almost trembling with excitement. Suddenly, Tom saw a robin fly out from the bushes. They both watched it go, and then Grandfather walked away. Tom asked, "Grandfather, what were you looking at in that bush?" Grandfather looked at Tom, confused, and said, "Why, the robin, Grandson." Tom's reply came quickly. "The robin? They're as common as dirt! It's just a robin." Grandfather looked even more incredulous. He drew a crude outline of a robin on the ground and asked, "Grandson, if it is *just* a robin, point out to me all thirty-eight black spots on that bird. And tell me, what are the two colors in a robin's eye that blend together to make a third distinct color?" He fired off question after question, none of which Tom had an answer for. Grandfather, a man in his late eighties with the passion for learning of a three-year-old, said, "Grandson, then it is not *just* a robin."

Upon hearing those words, my life, like Tom's, would never be the same again. I had spent enough time in the woods to have seen plenty of robins and to know what they were. Or at least I thought I did.

At first I was distraught. My whole world was crashing down around me. I was struggling to think of a single thing that I knew from my own experience to be true that wasn't so basic a child in kindergarten could tell you the answer. I remember looking at a pine tree a few feet away and thinking, "I guess I know the pine tree grows as a result of water and sunlight," and then berating myself because, although I knew a few fancy-sounding terms like *photosynthesis* and *coniferous*, I realized I knew next to nothing about pine trees from my own experience. And certainly not this pine tree—this magnificent individual before me. I didn't know what age it was, how much sunlight it liked, what its needles did under the weight of snow, which species of birds nested in its branches, if it was edible or medicinal, or what other gifts it possessed. I didn't know what its wood burned like, what it would be like to sleep on a bed of its needles, or as another living being, how I could communicate with it. Sure, some of the simplest questions I could answer by reading directly from a field guide, but that's just one person's view of pine trees in general. Depressed doesn't even begin to describe how I felt for weeks after this. I returned home to England, realizing I had wasted years of my life allowing other people to tell me what life is like. Yet I had not learned of anything beyond a label and a few tidbits of information that anyone could discover in a few minutes. In my own mind, I had learned nothing but merely to recite other people's opinions.

When I finally was able to accept my ignorance, it was like an epiphany. I felt as though I could see clearly for the first time in my life. I realized it is not important how *much* we know, but *how* we learn It's not important whether we reach the destination, but what experiences we have along the way. I realized that the world has more secrets to be discovered than I could possibly have time for. I began to look at life like a child in a candy shop. There was more to discover in my backyard than I had ever dreamed of. Now, what was previously "just" a pine tree has become a lifelong friend that every time I meet

I gaze upon as if I have never seen it before. (Which is true, because both the myself and the tree have changed since our last meeting.) I feel its needles, smell its bark, and watch how it changes as the seasons come and go. I feel its spirit as we sit together watching the birds flit around its branches. After years of experiencing pine trees for myself, I am happy to say that I am still only scratching the surface of understanding them; there is so much more. I think pine trees will keep me enthralled and elated until the day I die. A label tells you nothing; experiences discovering the soul of other living beings tell you everything.

Dylan and the Dinosaurs

An old friend of mine, Dylan, had a childhood that highlights perfectly the importance of the "need" to learn that stems not from trying to outcompete others but from the desires and passions of the soul. As a child he was a particularly poor speller of many words he came in contact with. He would regularly spell phonetically—how a word sounds. Instead of writing *when* he would spell it "wen," and instead of *the* he would write "thu." He did this for many years, as he explained, "… because they just weren't important to me. I never saw any reason to learn." It would be fair to say that the only need Dylan felt to spell correctly was the external pressure from teachers, and he remained extremely poor at spelling for a number of years. However, when asked to spell words that related to things he was passionate about it was a different world. He could not only spell them perfectly, but also with genuine enthusiasm, and then tell you anything you might wish to know about the things they described. For example, at five years old he could not spell *the* but could happily tell you how to spell *triceratops, dinosaur,* and *brontosaurus.*

Dylan still struggles with relatively basic spellings. But when he relates this story today, he explains how he worked so hard to remember how to spell those things he was passionate about—despite the difficulty—because he had an internal, soul-level need to know them. His passion fuelled his learning, and he experienced and used the words he learned because he valued them. We all have these pathways of passion toward learning; our role as adults is to identify them, encourage them, and honor them for each individual child.

TRULY ALIVE TIP

Creating Heroes

At around nine years old, the first hero I remember having was Kenny Dalglish. He wore the number 7 shirt for Liverpool Football Club. He was an attacking player who scored astonishing goals. When I played soccer in my youth with my friends, we would all choose which of our heroes we would like to be, and mine would always be Dalglish. Each of us would imitate our idols when we scored, copying their celebrations and doing our best to replicate their skills.

By the time I was in my early teens, my idol was John Lennon. I listened to his music everywhere I went and can still recite many of his lyrics. I wanted to be like him so badly that I started to learn the guitar. My most treasured possession was a huge book for the guitar with every single Beatles song in it. I think I must have worn the ink off the pages of that book, I used it so much.

And my last hero, whom I discovered in my adult life, was Grandfather Stalking Wolf who took his final walk many years before I learned of him. I was taught about his amazing life through Tom Brown Jr. Grandfather, as he was affectionately known, was a master of living in peace and harmony with the natural world. He was a Southern Lipan Apache who lived his whole life in freedom and happiness. Whenever I work on my nature skills, I try to think of how Grandfather would approach things, always striving to be like him, even if that is not physically possible.

I hope you are beginning to understand why I am telling you about my diverse heroes. I had a deep desire to be like them. They inspired and excited me, fuelling my passion to learn and discover life. To this day, they help me aspire to greatness, and I enjoy trying to emulate aspects of their being: Kenny's passion for something he loved, John's dedication to his beliefs, and Grandfather's ability to be free. We all have heroes, from our parents to people who are famous. The more we can tell stories to children about people who reached for the stars, who did amazing deeds, or who lived lives we admire, the more our children will also feel that desire to reach for greatness.

What Is Success?

A group of home-schooled boys, roughly aged seven to eleven, with whom some fellow instructors and I had the pleasure of spending a couple of years, taught us some great lessons about success. We had been mentoring them as part of our program for about a year, usually around once a month, when one of their most memorable lessons with us took place. They were always one of our more challenging groups because they were quick to argue with one another and could never seem to focus on one thing for very long.

On this particular day in early March, the weather was not being too kind to us. Slush, sleet, rain and near freezing temperatures prevailed—about the worst weather to be outside in for a whole day, especially with children. We planned to get a fire going with them, and then make coal-burned spoons (burn a depression in wood with coals, then scrape it clean).

The fire was started, and spoons were begun. As usual, after about fifteen minutes, many of the boys began to lose their focus and interest in the coal burning. Sensing this, we asked the children what they wanted to do, and the answer came almost unanimously that they wanted to keep the fire going more than they wanted to make the spoons. We were happy to oblige as the weather was making things a real challenge and keeping a fire going in the rain was a great skill to learn. We told them they would need to collect more firewood, and the words had barely left our mouths before they shot off into the woods, shouting to one another when they found good wood and organizing themselves into two and three-person groups. Their enthusiasm was good to see, but the best was yet to come.

One of the children shouted, "There's a big dry log over here," which, considering the weather, was a remarkable find. All the children gathered around the enormous log and began discussing how they could move it the hundred or so feet to the fire. At no point did they ask for help from us, which was unusual—only minutes before, some of them had asked us to make their spoons for them. It took them a while, but they finally worked out that if all eight of them could just lift the log into the air, they would be able to haul it over with it on their shoulders. So, remarkably, this group of boys who for a year had scarcely been able to play games together worked as a team and, with much grunting and groaning, brought the log to the fire.

Of course, we were impressed with their teamwork and fire-tending skills, but it was remarkable how successful *they* considered themselves to be. They did not need us to define and then pass judgment on their success. By deciding for themselves what was important for them, they had achieved far more than they would have with us directing their every move. This really brought them together as a group, gave them confidence, and allowed them to grow visibly in maturity. The children were still talking about that day more than a year later. You could hear the pride and sense of adventure and achievement in their voices. I am happy to say it had nothing to do with us as teachers.

Meeting Expectations

Even a brief look at the modern-day educational system shows that we are utterly obsessed with measuring progress and achieving a prescribed form of success. Children are tested, assessed and measured on a yearly, monthly, weekly, and even daily basis. It begins the moment they set foot into the school system and continues right through their high school and college lives. This can easily add up to over fifteen years of being constantly tested.

The system expects that a certain amount of progress be made each semester and year. If this expectation is not met, questions are asked of the student, and possibly the teacher. It is these two ideas, *success* and *progress*, that have driven education away from serving the individual. Nothing is wrong with either success or progress in and of themselves. The issue is that both have become so prescriptive and controlling that there is no room to maneuver for child or teacher. It is the way we elevate them to being the ultimate goal in any activity that is causing children pain. Our obsession with these ideas not only dominates the educational system but also ends up permeating children's lives outside school, at home and in society.

Because success and progress are so vehemently emphasized, children (and also adults) feel that they must constantly measure up. Failure is always hovering, and in this world "losers" are usually forgotten about, in many cases barely able to survive, economically, physically and spiritually.

The other major problem, that itself can be split into two parts, is expectation. First, children are constantly expected to live up to someone else's expectations and definitions of success. Worse, children come to expect to look to someone else to tell them what they should be doing. Neither of these is conducive to a peaceful mind or a creative one. Instead the result is that, as adults, we do not follow our own path, leaving us feeling lost and frustrated.

These two damaging effects alone would be bad enough. But it's not just children who have to conform to set requirements. In order to support this system, others have to jump through hoops that are equally controlling and limited in their vision. Teachers are assessed and graded regularly. Schools are inspected and in some places even organized into league tables or rankings. Of course, many feel that some level of accountability is necessary. But it is the nature of the current accountability that is particularly destructive because it is highly restrictive and based in fear. The repercussions of children failing tests can lead to schools being permanently shut down and teachers losing their jobs. There is only one path for children, teachers and educational establishments to walk—one where there is no time or space for "failure." The stakes are high, competition is fierce, and everyone knows it.

After the earliest years of a child's life, starting at about four or five years old, almost 100 percent of the tests and assessments they are subjected to are about knowledge. Generally this means the memorization and subsequent recollection of facts. Whether these tests are in the form of letters, numbers, or labels, it's all much the same: those children who meet the standards or exceed them receive the label "success." Those children who do not or cannot meet the standards are also given an official label: "failure." And what's really best for the system is if these people, these human beings, are simply ignored. After all, how could such a wondrous system possibly produce failures? Schools in some countries will often, in order to maintain their ranking and status, keep certain children from sitting exams. They do this if they think the child will receive a poor grade. So the child is denied the opportunity to achieve even the system's definition of success, let alone anyone else's.

The dysfunctional system of education is played out in a dysfunctional society. The students who fail these tests (which translates into "you *personally* are a failure") will often form the forgotten and neglected underclass of society. The students who do well in these tests (which translates into "you *personally* are a success") will often form the more affluent class of society. Many will fill roles of power and responsibility. As adults, then, why would those who have been deemed successful seek to change the educational system? After all, they have done very well by it. It is not difficult to reason that if others have failed, it must be their fault, not the system's.

Currently, an educational system is considered successful if it brings about greater financial wealth and security for both the individual and society. This is almost always in the form of more *doing*. Can we *do* 3 percent growth? Can we *do* lower unemployment? Can we *do* passing more tests? But what are children *being* while they are doing "success"? They are certainly not being more loving, peaceful, joyful or purposeful. A definition of success that only involves financial and material gain is itself very flimsy and completely lacking in depth. But bring in life's most basic truth, that we are all one, and there is no way this definition of success can stand up. Why would you choose to have more if it meant that someone else did not have enough simply to survive? Would you consider yourself successful, would you be happy, if the only reason you were rich was that the rest of your friends and family were living in poverty? Most of us would agree that success at the expense of others is not success, but this is undeniably what we are choosing. To remedy things, it is not about everyone having the same; it is about everyone simply being able to live with dignity. Wealth would still exist. Down and out and barely scraping together a life would not.

We each have the power and ability to make new choices, to re-define what we say is important. In this present moment we have a glorious opportunity to immerse our children in a different definition of success—one that leads to great freedom and love.

As individuals and as a society, we must find the strength and courage to give the gift of honoring that *individuals each define their own success*. We can give this gift by simply choosing to do so.

There will be people who object to this new definition of success and feel it goes too far. Yet it is not right to say that society is currently successful because it is able to provide a certain small percentage of the population with physical security. It should not be considered success if I eat a feast every night while ignoring the fact my brothers and sisters are starving.

The Nature of Testing

There is a world of difference between proving competency at a task and taking a test so someone else can label us a success or failure, thereby defining if we join the "winners" or "losers". So it is the nature of the assessments we give children that we should look deeply into. For example, if someone wanted to be a brain surgeon they would obviously have to take some sort of assessment to decide if they can operate on others. Anything else could be downright dangerous. But proving competency does not require children and young adults to be subjected to fifteen or more years of testing and labeling in an environ-ment where they know if they fail they could live in very real poverty, suffer ill-health and a distinct lack of opportunities to change their situation. A world like this can only exist when we believe ourselves to be separate from each other, constantly fighting to be that which we are and always will be: truly alive. We naturally want to know where children are in their understandings so we may serve them as best we can. But this can be done in a constructive, encouraging and loving environment.

In our new culture, failure will not be an option because there will be nothing to fail. No one can fail at life, so why are we checking constantly to see if children are? It is almost impossible to imagine the changes that this would bring about. Can you imagine learning something simply for the sheer joy of it? Can we even comprehend the satisfaction of learning because we are passionate about it, rather than because we fear failure in our lives if we do not?

The change would be monumental. Learning would be transformed overnight from an experience largely based in fear to a glorious expression of joy and love for life. This would in turn create peace and a sense of purpose for everyone.

CHAPTER 7

Education Becomes Experience

I do not teach anyone. I only provide the environment
in which they can learn.

~Albert Einstein

The Role of the Educator

We will later redefine our thinking about the roles of teacher and
student, but for now we will look at the role that teachers and communities must play if we are to lead children to experience a life of love,
peace, joy, and purpose. Our definition of teachers is not confined just
to those who stand at the front of a classroom. All adults are teachers,
regardless of their label.

Let's recap the main points:

- We are all one. There is no separation.
- We are more than body and mind; we are also a soul.
- Education exists for the free and full expression of the individual.
- Every child is unique.
- Individuals each define their own success.

This redefinition of the basic assumptions about the way we lead children to interact with life naturally leads us to question the role the teacher will play. With so much emphasis on child-driven learning, will there even be a role for the traditional teacher anymore? The reality is that this new culture will put a huge emphasis on the quality of the educational experience. Teaching will take place at a depth and with a richness not previously possible.

The two roles that adults can play are simple:

- Establish within the student a deep love of learning and of life itself.
- Provide opportunities for full exploration and experience of the self and of life.

The teacher will, in effect, become a *facilitator of experiences*. Teachers' first priority will be to facilitate children turning on to life. The only thing that it is vital for children to learn is that learning equals adventure and brings excitement, satisfaction, and a sense of purpose to their life experience. How is this done? Simply by not only allowing but encouraging children to follow and explore their unique passions. By becoming aware of children's inherent desire for discovery, we can nurture it to form the basis for lifelong learning. When this is in place, we will find that we are no longer fighting against children. A more organic and natural flow occurs because we are working with life (our soul), not against it.

As children are exposed to new experiences and opportunities, they themselves will ultimately determine the direction and nature of their "education." Who knows what direction they will take? One thing for certain is that they will not continue in the direction we are currently going. In many regards, teachers will take a step back; they will not be forcing children to go in a predetermined direction. However, the manner of their influence will become multilayered and multifaceted. These different roles will require teachers to know each child far more intimately than is currently the case. The relationship will change from merely being a funnel for information to one that sees teachers striving to lead children to discover their own independent experiences of love, peace, joy, and purpose.

There will of course be influences from society. Children will look to us, just as we looked to our parents to guide and inspire us. As they see adults being, for example, excited, peaceful, confident, empathic and compassionate, children will naturally also pursue similar experiences. Just because we are giving children far more freedom in their lives does not mean that society will become unrecognizable overnight.

When running classes for adults or training staff in how to help children reconnect with nature, I always use a phrase that is vital for us to understand. "Let them see what you have become." If I am attempting to teach a child, particularly a teenager, a new skill, you can bet they are thinking, be it consciously or unconsciously, "If I learn this skill, is this the kind of person I will become?" When I think about my heroes, I wanted to be like Kenny Dalglish not only for his soccer skills but because he had (and still has) the most amazing joy in his eyes when he is anywhere near a soccer field. I wanted that joy in my life. I wanted to be like John Lennon, not only because he could play the guitar, but because he seemed to me to have a deep purpose and sense of peace that I wanted to experience for myself. And now I want to be like Grandfather Stalking Wolf, not because of his impressive survival skills, but because he had a love for life that makes me passionate to walk a similar path. I was not so much interested in what my heroes could do, I was inspired by who they were being.

I am not surprised that children are resisting learning much of what we are trying to teach them. When they look at most adults, what do you think they believe they will become? A large part of what children see in the adult world is constant fighting, living in fear and deep apathy. Imagine you are seven years old. Switch on the evening news or read any newspaper. Would you want to become part of that world?

We currently teach children that success comes from external sources—money, house, car, other possessions, career—and that for extra happiness we should ensure they are bigger, better, faster, and that we have more of everything. This obviously has hugely negative implications for what children will seek later in life. They are currently required to memorize facts and knowledge from external sources, either from something or somebody. They are taught that is it fine to take on someone else's truth through external knowledge acquisition, not their own truth through personal experience. Unfortunately, the resulting "success," gained by external means, is not a measure of who we truly are. We are not our knowledge or our grades and we are not our money. Nor are we our house, our possessions, or even our career. Just because we worship these as a society does not mean that they bring us everlasting happiness and peace. Indeed, the exact opposite is quite often true. The adulation of these things can lead far, far away from being truly alive because they are all found externally, not internally. They are not what and who we are. For education to be successful in providing all the things we desire in our hearts, it has to support children internally. And the only way to move it inward is if it becomes a personal experience.

This is a good point at which we can drop the word *education* and replace it with *experience*. This shift in perspective allows for crucial changes to education in both the journey and the goal. First, it changes the goal from being a vision of distant success at some point in the future to enjoying the experience of the present moment—which, as we have seen, is the only place we are truly alive. It also changes who is in control of the journey. The educational experience moves from a source external to the learner to one that is guided by the individual child. There is nothing the child has to do, so there is everything they can be. It is so difficult to *be* loving while you are concentrating on *doing* a hundred things that someone else tells you to.

By coming together and creating shared experiences we shift our whole focus away from adult-dictated material worship, to child-initiated honoring of the soul, with adults as the humble facilitators of this magnificent process.

The Dance of Experience

We come now to what we will call the *dance*. The most effective teachers are constantly learning from their pupils, and in many cases they learn more from their pupils than their pupils learn from them. The teacher should always be asking questions, always striving to understand more deeply both themselves and those they are trying to support. At any time in the teacher-pupil relationship, we can ask, who is the teacher, and who is the pupil? Really, this is just a matter of perspective. Now, as we move away from traditional education and consider experience as a better description of what is occurring, it is obvious to see that the teacher/facilitator and pupil are both always experiencing. This is where the magnificent dance happens. Sometimes the teacher is leading, guiding both individuals to new experiences. Other times the pupil may be leading. At times neither is leading and the lines become blurred as both walk into unknown experiences hand in hand. Initially, the teacher must lead the child to take the first steps along a certain path, but after that who is to say what will happen? Where will it lead? The possibilities are, of course, infinite.

Let's illustrate this with an example of a girl having a passion to learn how to grow her own food. She works with a facilitator who is knowledgeable but, more importantly, also highly passionate about plants and gardening. In the initial experiences, the facilitator will lead the dance, perhaps starting by showing the girl plants to grow and leading her to an experience centered on soil quality. After spending some time in the garden, the girl would gain in both knowledge and wisdom. Very soon, as a result of her experiences, she would begin to ask her own questions. It is at this point that the girl may well become the leader of the dance. She will probably ask some questions that the facilitator never even considered. In this way, the student is then leading the facilitator in the dance to new experiences. If they come across a question that neither knows the answer to, and try to discover all they can together, then neither is leading the dance. What a beautiful way to learn and to experience life freely and fully.

Making a comparison with the modern-day system is easy, using the analogy of the dance. The current system decides in advance what music is to be played, when and where the dance will take place, who will be dancing, and what the dance will be. All the pupil has to do is follow in the footsteps and shadow of the teacher. Simple? Of course. It's simply the most uncreative and uninspiring thing you can ask a creative being to do.

Our new model of the dance is highly organic and allows the music to be created as the dance is taking place. It takes place as both facilitator and pupil feel inspired and the dance itself flows naturally from the joy of being free.

Experience is simply something happening in the present moment. Unlike what our present system teaches children, an experience is never "right" or "wrong." It only has the meaning that each individual gives it in the present moment. Naturally, facilitators will want to give children what they consider to be the most fulfilling experiences, but children should never be graded or judged on how they respond. From here on, we will often use the term *experience* in favor of *education*. It is fuller, holds more possibilities, and honors the unique creative energy of each individual.

As a life of love, peace, joy, and purpose is experienced internally, these qualities will be manifested in the outside world. True educational experiences start from within.

TRULY ALIVE TIP 🌿🌿🌿🌿🌿🌿

Fox Walking

By supporting children in the way they physically move, we can positively affect the actions of the child and the choices of humanity. Walking is such an integral part of life that it plays a central role in helping to create our thoughts and beliefs. The way that most of us walk around is not particularly conducive to peaceful experiences. We walk quickly, rushed even, and in most cases the sole purpose of our movement is to get from A to B, as fast as possible—no different to our lives. The destination is considered more important than the experience.

It is easy to observe a direct correlation between the way we walk and our relationship with life. If we walk quickly and are hurried, pounding each step into the ground, our interactions with life are unlikely to be gentle, loving and peaceful. But if we walk as though every step is a prayer, in return, life will bless each footfall, bringing us inner peace and confidence.

To find a way of walking that promotes a balance of body, mind and spirit, we turn to fox walking. We can still walk to get from A to B, but with fox walking we connect with life at every step. This is a different philosophy, where the experience becomes more important than the destination.

A good way to explain fox walking is to describe what it is not. When most of us in modern-day society walk we strike the ground with our heel first. And it should be emphasized that it is most definitely a strike, a hit. What is happening to our being? Our physical body jars as the heel strikes. As we pitch our body forward, eager to get somewhere, our mind is usually worrying about what is going to happen in the future, and as a result we walk too fast, too distracted to move our focus away from our small reality where we are all separate, needing to run faster than the next person to stay ahead. We move at the fast pace of our cities, which do not support our full being because they take us away from our true connection with the Earth.

Fox walking slows us down. When we learn to enjoy the experience of walking rather than being constantly desperate to get somewhere, we can celebrate life where we are, in the present moment.

To fox walk, bring the outside ball of your foot down first, placing it gently on the ground. Roll inward so that the inside ball of your foot is also in contact with the ground. Then allow your toes and heel to find their place on the Earth. Finally, shift your weight forward. This is the human version of how a fox walks, silently placing one paw down after the other. If you are still unsure of how to fox walk, imagine that you are stepping on a living thing. Step gently, and give gratitude that you are supported and loved by the Earth.

We often complain of having no time to ourselves—no time to find peace. I recall a mentor of mine, Rick Berry, once saying to me, "Remember, fox walking isn't just a way of walking; it's a way of living!" Indeed, it is almost impossible to fox walk and not feel peaceful and connected to all that is. If we can share this with children, it will transform their life experience.

A note of caution here: Walking slowly can be excruciating. Not for the body, but for the mind that is screaming, "Do something! Do anything! Go faster!" As with all suggestions for creating a more peaceful life, this simply shows us how deep our ruts have become. It's okay. If you are doing this with children, turn it into a game, where they have to be very quiet and slow. Make sure fox walking is a positive experience, not a chore. If that means ten seconds is the maximum time of the experience, that's fine. Try including it as part of your daily rituals for even a few moments, and you and your children will become more connected with life and more connected with each other.

Who Enables Experience?

In response to this question, we will explore two aspects—societal and individual—of who should enable a free and full culture. It is difficult to make direct comparisons with our current system, as we are not comparing like with like. Nevertheless, it will be evident where changes are taking place.

Our present model is largely dictated at the national (or state) level. That is to say, each country's government—French, Norwegian, Canadian, American, etc.—decides what and how they will teach children. Education provided in one area of a country is generally expected to be the same in any other area. This has enabled a standardized system to function. Test results in one area of the country are of equal value to those anywhere else. However, this has meant that education has been largely homogenized, and, sadly, it is rapidly doing the same to children's lives. It is simply not necessary, nor is it advisable, for us to look for the energy and love of the truly alive culture to stem from a government at the national or state level. Instead, the energy and passion to provide children with a free and full life experience must come from the *community* around the child. In every community in the world, there are people with passion, great knowledge, and infinite wisdom. This will not change. In fact, the new culture will allow teaching to become far richer, wider ranging, and deeper reaching. It will allow a great many more adults to take part in the dance of teaching, learning from, and walking hand in hand with children, than has previously been possible.

What does *community* in this context mean? Community in the context of a free and full culture is left open to interpretation, depending on the needs and choices of each individual. It could be very narrow, very broad, or any combination. For example, your community could mean you and your children. It could include grandparents, aunts, or uncles. Perhaps it means your geographical community—the neighborhood, town or city. Perhaps it means your cultural family—your interests, religion, or beliefs. Maybe it means your country as a whole. Possibly it's like-minded friends. Maybe it's a little bit from each of the above. The ideal scenario is one where your community will provide opportunities for children to fully discover and experience themselves and the world around them.

Naturally, the greater the diversity of opportunities, the richer the life experience will be for children. All these different communities provide vastly different pathways for the free and full expression of the individual. Here are some examples:

A community of rock climbers could create an amazing space for children to experience scaling a cliff face for themselves. The community of the town is not likely to be able to do so with the same degree of passion, knowledge, and opportunity for hands-on experience. In contrast, the community of the town could provide an opportunity for children to undertake an art project, for example, where creativity is experienced on a larger scale than the community of rock climbers could provide.

Similarly, the national community could offer the chance to live in a different country or on another continent. A number of individuals could experience life in a new way that the community of immediate family may not be able to provide. Conversely, the community of family may provide the opportunity for a child to experience love that the national community is unable to do to the same degree.

TRULY ALIVE TIP

The Journey or the Goal?

Only one of these happens in the present moment, so only one of these is real. Of course, it's the journey: the here-and-now experience. Goals and aspirations are wonderful—everybody needs them—but they should not be confused with what is actually real, and that is the experience of the here and now. If we only ever give children praise for achieving the final goal, they will obviously grow up thinking that is the only thing that is important. They will likely be unhappy if they don't reach the goal, and may even consider themselves a failure if it doesn't happen exactly the way they had planned. Not many adults—possibly none—can say that they met all their goals in the exact way they planned. Modern society is full of unhappy goal chasers. Yet we have already seen that no one can fail at life, and so it is important to give praise for the child's journey. Praise should be given equally for their passion, their "mistakes," their joyful thoughts, their loving and peaceful actions large and small, and even for just being alive. All of these are successes and worthy of the highest adulation.

Community Transformed

Everyone has something they can share to enrich the lives of our youth. We are all passionate about something in our lives. We each have knowledge and wisdom that could help someone else. I imagine that right now, as you are reading this, you can think of something you are passionate, knowledgeable, or wise about. It doesn't matter how large or small or how important or insignificant you consider it to be. To a child it could be life-changing. It could be the most magnificent gift they ever receive.

In this new culture, community becomes multifaceted and multi-layered. We are not reliant on one source, the government, to provide guidance on life to our children. The truly alive culture creates an ever-changing tapestry rich with adventure and possibility. The opportunity emerges not just for children to experience life but for every layer of community to play a meaningful part in society. Parents may wish to assist children in their process of choosing experiences by helping them to understand the options before them. This support is especially important in children's early years when they are not yet fully independent in their decision making.

The question then becomes, who in that community should be a facilitator for these experiences to be placed in front of children? Quite simply, anyone who is willing or able and chooses to do so. Above all, it should be anyone who is passionate about the experience they are seeking to facilitate.

So many people have so much to share—carpenters, poets, mathematicians, hunters, engineers, artists—the list is endless. Let them all share their passions so that children may learn first hand from them. Imagine learning all the time from people who are deeply passionate about their subject. What a joy. And what an opportunity.

Hundreds and even thousands of people reading this may be inspired to share with children their knowledge, wisdom and passion.

What would you want to share? What would you want to help children experience in this world?

Can you imagine the excitement and wonder a child would feel, surfing the Internet, exploring what different communities have to offer, and finding more things to inspire them than they could possibly have time for in a whole life? This is education. This is discovering the secrets of the universe. This is the way to create lifelong, independent learners.

With our new understandings we can transform our communities to play the role they were intended to: supporting each other, and facilitating opportunities for our children to experience the free and full expression of their being. There will naturally be many different types of communities and many layers to each community. From there, the roles of the parent and child will be to work together to choose experiences based on the desires and passions of each child.

Charlie's Gift

In guiding children and families to reconnect with nature, I have been fortunate to come into contact with many remarkable people. Many adults volunteer their time at programs we run. Each of them has a different kind of skill to impart. People offer their support by making beautiful food, teaching skills, or helping out with paperwork.

One of the most remarkable volunteers we had was a middle-aged man named Charlie. He was with us for a class we ran for teens that lasted just under two weeks. He came to volunteer to help us with, in his words, "Anything that needed doing." Many of us were friends with Charlie before he came, and knew that he had some great outdoor skills, mainly due to his living half in society and half as what many might term a "mountain man." Probably as a result of not spending much time in what most would consider ordinary environments, he was socially awkward around groups of people and certainly stuck out as different. Many people avoided him because of this. Charlie was not used to teaching, and in particular he didn't believe that anybody would want to learn from him. We let him settle in for a few days, and when he was a little more relaxed I asked him to lead an activity playing games with the children. He was understandably uncomfortable and asked if there was anything else he could do. "Sure," I said. "Why don't you tell the children some stories about the way you live?" After all, his mountain-man lifestyle was unique. He reluctantly agreed to this.

I came down just after lunch to find the children hanging on Charlie's every word. He was telling them about the tools he made in order to live the way he did and stories about amazing and inspiring things he had done that staff were still talking about years later. His gift to those children was to allow them into a world so different to their version of reality that none of them knew it even existed. Charlie was so popular that we cancelled what we had planned for the next day due to overwhelming demand for more of his stories and insight into his unique life. He was utterly surprised at the children's interest, but clearly very happy to have contributed so richly to their development. Charlie, like all of us, has a gift, and he shared it generously.

A wonderfully powerful way to consciously create change is to acknowledge that *everyone has a gift to give, to themselves, their communities, and to life.*

Teacher–Pupil Ratio

The ratio of teacher to pupil is important because it plays a large role in the nature of the experiences we can share with children. In most cases, a smaller teacher–pupil ratio positively affects the depth and the richness of the student's experience.

A "normal" ratio in the classroom of most developed countries can range anywhere from 1:10 to 1:40. That is, one teacher for anywhere between ten and forty children. In developing countries, this can shoot up to around eighty children for one teacher. The classes in England I taught rarely had fewer than twenty-eight children in them; the norm was thirty. Quite obviously, this limits the amount of personal attention that any individual child receives. In fact, children in school settings receive literally minutes and seconds of individual attention each day. It is a sad indictment of our society that we have allowed this to happen. It is no wonder the education system struggles to produce children who are able to do much more than simple memorization of external facts (though this is not really a problem for the system itself because that is the goal anyway). It also severely limits the type of experiences teachers can share with children. It is very difficult to provide hands-on experiences for thirty or so children. But with a teacher–student ratio of that proportion, it is relatively easy to get children to remember facts. And, hey presto! The limitations are set.

Again, what we are seeking here is a balance. To have every educational experience in a large group setting is clearly not healthy. But equally, the same could be said of having every educational experience in a one-on-one setting. An ideal situation for a child would be to have some experiences in a large group, some in a small group, and others in an individual setting. No two children's personalities are the same, and they all learn in completely different ways. Some learn well in large groups; some prefer to learn in the company of just one or two other people. Again, we are seeking to provide experiences that will lead to the strongest love, the greatest peace, the most joy, and the deepest purpose.

In most cases where there is a large number of pupils for each teacher, a damaging cycle is created. As an elementary school teacher I experienced this repeatedly, and it is very difficult, if not almost impossible, to avoid. The pupils, because they naturally seek excitement, adventure, and to discover the world around them, look for attention in order to be supported in experiencing these. When the teacher, because of sheer numbers of children is unable to give what is needed, children begin to misbehave, sometimes to alleviate boredom, and sometimes as a cry to communicate that they need to experience more, that they are not fulfilled. Because pupils are misbehaving, the teacher has to stop what little teaching has been going on and take time to control the class. But then, there is even less to occupy the restless minds of children, and so they misbehave to a larger degree. Or worse still, if they are not the kind to misbehave, they simply turn off. Boredom makes children (and adults for that matter) want either to rebel or completely turn off. Both are utter disasters for a child's learning and life experiences. It is a situation that our current education system excels at creating, yet fails to address.

To get an idea of what the benefits of a low pupil–teacher ratio might be, we'll go back to the example of children being given the opportunity to rock climb. Let's take a look at the experience of a child in two different scenarios, first, where there is a 1:15 ratio, and second, where there is a 1:1 ratio (that is, children having their own individual teacher).

1:15 Scenario:

Everyone sits down at the base of the cliff. The climbing instructor discusses what is going to happen and goes over safety points. A number of children ask questions, which takes up some time. All the children are understandably itching to go climbing. A line is formed to decide the order in which the children will climb. There is some jostling and competition as everyone would like to be at the head of the line, because everyone is entrenched in the model of "there's not enough"—in this case, time and resources. The first child is strapped into the safety harness. He gets some answers to questions about the equipment that were not covered earlier, and finally he is off. He starts to climb with the instructor. The child feels nervous at first, but soon becomes more confident. He feels he can trust his body to pull him ever upward. Maybe he can even get to the top. Just as he begins to truly enjoy the experience, he is dismayed to find that it is the next person's turn. Down to the ground he goes, happy for the experience but frustrated because he wanted to explore more. Still, it was a good thing to *do*.

1:1 Scenario:

Now let's move to the child who has her own individual teacher. The teacher explains basic techniques and goes over climbing safety. The child asks questions to clarify her understanding. Then, up onto the cliff face they both go. At first the girl is nervous, but soon she begins to become more confident. She feels she can trust her body to pull her ever upward. Maybe she could even reach the top. As they climb a few more steps, the teacher refines the girl's technique, and she feels a true understanding as the suggestion is put into practice. They have been climbing for some time now. The girl begins to develop a connection with the rock. She and her teacher stop to admire its beauty. There is no rush. Farther and farther they climb. The child's legs and arms are tired, but the rock is now a friend: a relationship has begun. It is a wondrous experience. As the girl nears the top, she looks down and sees how far they've come. She looks left and right and sees cliff faces for miles around. She sees possibility and imagines new experiences—so much more to climb. And then, she has a sudden awareness that, with her final push, the utter joy she is feeling is not because she has reached the top, but because of the incredible experience along the way. Her senses have been awakened. She's never felt like that before—so peaceful, so full of adventure and so truly alive. She is in love with rock climbing, and discovers that her purpose is to feel freedom on those magnificent cliff faces. What a thing to *be*. It might just be a different reality. It is certainly a different experience.

As we've discussed, this is not meant to suggest that every moment of learning should be provided in a one-on-one setting. What this is meant to illustrate is that trying to teach children en masse can be highly limiting for pupil and teacher alike. It is limiting not only on a *doing* level, but also on a *being* level. The children in the large class gets to physically *do* less. But, more importantly, they get to *be* less. There is far less opportunity for them to experience all aspects of their being: the body, the mind, and crucially, the forgotten part—the soul. The depth of the experience is in real danger of never going beyond the surface. Thus, as we grow into adults, we create a whole society that rarely goes beneath the surface of anything; everything is a purely physical, doing act. Instead, if it is appropriate to the experience, whenever possible we should seek to give children as much individual attention as possible. The experience will be richer for everyone—teachers and pupils alike.

Where Will Experience Take Place?

If we stay with the idea that wherever possible children should gain as much hands-on experience of life as possible, then we have really already answered this question. Experiences should of course be in the places where life is actually happening. If a child wants to experience how to throw a baseball, what better place than on the baseball diamond? A video game doesn't offer anything near the richness of experience of holding the ball, and feeling every muscle in the body move to throw it fast and accurately. If children want to understand the behavior of a deer, what better place than in a forest? The merits of a book pale into insignificance when compared to interacting with another life form, observing it respond to the subtlest of nuances in its environment.

It is hard to make a case for children to sit in a classroom all day.

What is there to inspire them inside a modern-day school? I don't mean something to grab their attention for a few minutes; I mean something really to inspire them and get them excited about just being alive. It is a worryingly short list. The indoor classroom is not conducive to providing the types of hands-on experience that lead to the development of *being*-ness in a child.

The world is infinitely richer outdoors, filled with constant stimuli, offering never-ending lessons. You can never stop learning while being outside and just observing.

When we start asking deep questions, we find that there is very little reason why children should be educated entirely inside school buildings. There they are shut off from natural stimuli and a more spontaneous, authentic experience of life. It is no surprise that so many children find school an altogether uninspiring part of their lives. It offers precious little opportunity to be truly alive.

Cross Generational Learning

In most schools (particularly larger ones) children are permanently segregated into narrow groups dependent on their age. For example, all the eleven-year-olds are together in one class and separated from every other age group. This is obviously because most of them are at similar learning levels in terms of their brain development. Yet when they only ever interact with this one age group it almost seems like a factory production line. Educational opportunities provided by different communities would naturally expose children to a diversity of ages and experiences. Providing this type of learning would add a richness and depth to a child's life and would release them from their current narrow, restricting form of education.

By far the most successful and enriching experiences I have personally been able to offer children have been when I have intentionally created a larger community—or tribe. The word tribe is used because this accurately paints an image of all ages coming together. Elders who are seventy and eighty years old live, play, and learn alongside the seven- and eight-year-old children. Families and all ages interact and play together. But here is the crucial part: everybody can and does teach everybody else. One of my favorite things to do is to give teens responsibility for teaching younger children the skills they as teens have recently acquired. It is amazing to see different dynamics from the traditional adult–child model, and usually it works remarkably well. The elders, as teachers and facilitators, do not just pass on knowledge; they share the thing we all need to learn most—wisdom. Personal experience is always many times more powerful than simply listening to information, and the elders have it in abundance, gathered over the decades of their lives. It is little wonder our society has major problems with wisdom—those who have it are marginalized by retirement. They are given little chance to contribute their vast stores of wisdom. Having seen the results with my own eyes, I know the most powerful way for children to discover life is as part of a cross-generational community. Just because as a society we have lost this does not mean we cannot choose to regain it. Like all the other positive environments, if it is something we truly wish to create, it is simply a choice away.

CHAPTER 8

A New Time

We are always getting ready to live but never living.

~Ralph Waldo Emerson

Time, Destination and Expectation

Late one summer, I travelled to the woods and mountains of New Hampshire. My wife Kat and I were off for some adventures, putting some of our survival skills to the test. We had with us some basics—a knife, a water bottle, some beef jerky—certainly enough tools and food to last us weeks and months, well past the week or so we had put aside. I had never seen the mountains of New Hampshire before, though I had heard wonderful things about them from many people. I wasn't disappointed. As soon as we stepped into the wilderness, I had to stop to marvel at the forests of beech trees that had dropped their leaves the previous fall, leaving a rich, brown carpet on the forest

117

floor. Their canopies were thick with leaves, and the sunlight pushed through to create a magical, dappled light all around us. The smell was unmistakably one of summer. Hot but cool beneath the trees. All around us life was in full swing.

Our only plan was to go without three things. We would give up three anchors almost all of us permanently drag around—anchors so heavy we do not realize what a weight and a burden they are to our souls until we can free ourselves of them. They are time, destination, and expectation. We knew we had to be back in a week or so, we knew we would be somewhere in these woods, and, as for expectations, mine didn't go beyond hoping to catch a glimpse of a moose. We made shelters from the feather-soft beech leaves, which kept us warm, dry, and happy. We caught some fish and a few snakes, found plenty of wild edible plants, went tracking, and simply followed our hearts. Life was good.

After about halfway through the first day, I could feel my mind slowing down, letting go of its self-importance, and getting back in harmony with the natural rhythms of the Earth. Kat and I hardly spoke more than a few words each day to each other. Not because we had fallen out, but because we understood each other without speaking. I was so content with being plugged back in to the flow of the world around me that I didn't feel the need to fill the silence with anything. We had no time to keep, nowhere to go, and nothing that needed to happen. It was the kind of journey that didn't have a destination. That is a rare thing in our 100-mph society. I was grateful to be enjoying a different reality.

I was close to sleep on the second night when a life-changing event happened. I do not believe I could have experienced such beauty without letting go of those three anchors, those balls-and-chains of our own making: time, destination and expectation. At first I thought a number of people were coming toward our small camp area, singing joyously. My eyes opened quickly and I half expected this group of people to walk right up to our shelter. But the noise never came any closer nor moved farther away. It was a wondrous sound, like fifty people all singing in unison, just far enough away that I couldn't make out the words. I listened for hours, riveted by the sound. I had never experienced something like this before. If a sound could ever invoke a feeling of love and freedom, it was this one. The gentle singing, the rising and falling melodies, continued for hours. After I had been listening, captivated for some time, I remembered a conversation I'd had with a Native American friend of mine, Juan. He had told me that the mountains had once sung in his presence, at a time when he was very still and peaceful. He too had wondered what it could have been at first, so late at night and so deep in the woods. When he returned, he asked some of the elders what it could have been, and they said what he had felt was right, that the mountains had indeed been singing— "thrumming" was the term he used. I heard those sweet, melodious voices every night in New Hampshire after that. I tried to stay awake for as long as I could, completely enthralled by the feeling, the magic, and the majesty of it.

Most of us never let go those three heavy anchors—time, destination, and expectation—that keep us locked in our world of separation and fear. We cling to them for dear life, thinking that if we do not have them around us life will somehow shatter like a pane of glass into a million pieces and fall to the floor. Nothing could be further from the truth. The only thing that may shatter is our illusion that we know what reality is. I have since heard what I believe is the voice of the mountains in a number of different places. It has always talked to the very core of me—my soul. But it has never happened while I have been running around at 100-mph, with somewhere to go, something to do, and busily worrying about yesterday, tomorrow, and how I can "get ahead." Those mountains in New Hampshire taught me more with their singing than I learned throughout my entire time in regular education. They inspired me to want to be a better person, to discover the secrets of nature, to care for my fellow humans, and to rearrange my thinking about what is actually alive—none of which I experienced in almost two decades of "proper" education. They showed me the doorway to quite literally a different reality, but most of all they showed me what happens when we allow ourselves simply to *be*.

TRULY ALIVE TIP

Turn Routine into Ritual

Getting out of as many routines as possible is very healthy. Yet every day, our lifestyles dictate we follow some sort of rhythm. In one way or another, we all have to take care of our most basic needs: food, water, housing, hygiene, and so on. Attending to these can easily create routines that, when repeated over long periods of time, become ruts. It's particularly these deep ruts we should do our utmost to keep children from falling into.

Ruts mean we are not living with very little consciousness of the present moment. We become as if on 'auto-pilot', asleep at the wheel. Thich Nhat Hanh says that, "Some people say that only walking on burning coals or walking on spikes or on water are miracles, but I find that simply walking on the Earth is a miracle." We must ask ourselves if we are going through life on auto-pilot, or if we are able to enjoy the miracles of the present moment. Are we truly alive as we walk, as we eat and go about our daily business? The opportunity is there for us and for our children in every moment, but it depends completely on our point of view. One of the most effective ways to do that is to turn routines into rituals. This means that whatever activity we are doing, we change our mindset from, "This is a chore and I wish I didn't have to do it," to "This is a pleasure, an act of worship or gratitude, that allows me to be more connected to life." It sounds simplistic, but it really is that easy. It's a matter of choosing what we focus on and changing our perception.

Let's use doing the dishes as an example. We can perceive this task as a boring chore: one that takes up our time, and every time we even think about it, let alone do it, we find ourselves frustrated and even angry. If we can find just one positive thing about it and focus upon that we can turn it into a ritual. We may choose to enjoy the experience of water on our hands, and we give thanks for the pleasure it brings. Or we may choose to enjoy the experience of service for our family. You will likely choose something that increases one or more of your feelings of love, peace, joy, or purpose. There are hundreds of routines that with the simplest of choices we can turn into rituals. Instead of detracting from our experience of life, these rituals actually enhance it.

When Will Experience Take Place?

There is a time that seems not to exist in the modern-day education system. It is hard to say where it has gone. It appears to have been lost, discarded, or filed away in a dusty cupboard somewhere. It became lost so long ago that children have almost forgotten it even exists. It is the time we rediscovered at the start of this book—the here and now, the *present moment*.

As we begin consciously to create change that leads our children to experience their connection with life, the current routines of the modern education system and society will not only fall away, they will simply become impossible to maintain.

For a religious person of a particular denomination, the time to go to their place of worship may be at a certain time or on a given day, but it is likely they understand that every day, each moment—not just their visit to their place of worship—is a sacred one. Similarly, if we are seeking for our children to be truly alive, every moment is a golden opportunity for discovery. Each second is filled with the possibility of love, peace, joy, and purpose. Therefore, how can we say that learning experiences can only take place between the hours of 9:00 a.m. to 3:00 p.m. Monday to Friday, or whatever the specific routines are in your part of the world?

The education system lives perennially in the future. Children always have a distant goal to reach, almost always in the form of a test to pass sometime in the future. Children work immensely hard, they memorize a multitude of facts, they pass or fail the test, and then there's the next one, and the next one. They always have something to worry about, something to preoccupy them that prevents them from living in the present. Goodness only knows what children might do if we allowed them to live in the here and now. They just might figure out that they are a *soul* and that all the tests and facts presented before them are rather pointless in comparison to embracing their true identity. No government directives or actions could maintain our current systems in the face of such power.

The present is where the *soul* is experienced. However, it is hard for children to discover this if they are constantly worrying about tests or about what pitfalls may await them in the future. If we truly wish for our children to reconnect with all that is, we must acknowledge that life is happening right now, not when they achieve someone else's definition of success.

As we shift the focus from teacher-driven to child-directed experiences, we must leave the rigidity and routines of the current system behind. Routines diminish the soul. Or, to put it more accurately, they diminish the awareness that we have of being a soul. Routines as strict as the school system force children to shrink back into their mind and body. As they do so a whole world is left behind. A universe of opportunities and experiences is shut down. A life of routines, rigidity, and planning is a long way from the optimal environment in which a creative soul can flourish. So are standing in lines, being quiet, sitting for hours, following rules—same thing, same time, same day—following someone else's idea of a life and, worst of all, the constant routine of being placed in an environment full of fear; the constant unstated admonition that "You'd better not fail."

Think of the routines we have, day after day. They are almost always controlled by either one of two sources, both external to us: *time* and the *rules of society*, both spoken and unspoken. Here's a typical day of routine in the life of a child:

They wake up at the same time each morning to the shock of an alarm clock. They dress, eat, and go to school, same time each day, same days each week. They sit in the same seat, and use the same books to "learn" from until the bell sounds, and then they are allowed to play, go to the bathroom and eat. Another bell sounds and they are quiet, awaiting instruction. They take a test in silence in order to prove they are not failing. Another bell sounds and they return home for the day, ready to do it all again in the morning. This time of "discovery," of laying the best possible foundations for adult life, lasts for at least eleven years. If a child is really "successful," it might go on for twenty.

Spontaneity, creativity, and following one's heart: *these* are talking the soul's language. It is through these that a greater balance between the soul, the mind, and the body can be achieved. As children who embrace and follow these feelings grow into young adults, they create and experience life in a balanced, healthy way because they themselves are balanced. A life of love, peace, joy, and purpose becomes a reality, not a dream.

Encouraging the next generation to live right here, and right now, in the present, does not mean that we cannot make plans. For example, a child might choose to spend three months experiencing being an artist, learning from a master. This would be likely to require planning and thinking about the future. But while immersed in the experience itself, there is nothing at which to fail. Free from our expectations, the child would be free to experience the fullness of being an artist in the present moment and, through this, to experience being truly alive.

As individuals and as a society, we must find the strength and courage to give the gift of honoring that *life happens in the present moment*. We can give this gift by simply choosing to do so.

CHAPTER 9

Independent Learners and Lovers of Life

If we value independence, if we are disturbed by the growing
conformity of knowledge, of values, of attitudes, which our
present system induces, then we may wish to set up conditions
of learning which make for uniqueness,
for self-direction, and for self-initiated learning.

~Carl Rogers

Fire Making With Stalking Wolf

I would like to relate a wonderful story that was told to me by Tom
Brown Jr. about becoming independent. The three people in this story
are Tom, his friend Rick (both around eight years old at the time), and
Stalking Wolf, or "Grandfather".

Tom and Rick met Grandfather when they were very young, and they were amazed at how he lived, in the woods, close to nature, reliant on his superb skills for everything he needed. From the stories I have heard Tom tell about Grandfather, he was happier than any person I have ever met.

The two young boys were fascinated to learn how Grandfather could live so easily and so well without all the modern amenities they were used to, so they asked the old Apache to share his knowledge with them. They knew he made fire because there was often one burning in his camp, but they had never seen how he did it. They also knew he did not use any tools from modern society because he would permit none of these in his camp. They desperately wanted to know the secret of fire making, and Grandfather used their need to know to guide the two boys not just toward learning, but to complete independence. Here's how he did it.

Tom and Rick finished school for the day and headed into the woods to see Grandfather. When they were in sight of his camp, they saw him, kneeling down, body moving, and smoke billowing out from near his foot in front of him. They were amazed. They had never seen anything like this before, and rushed to Grandfather to ask him if this was how he made fire. Whatever Grandfather had used to produce the smoke he quickly stuffed into a bag, and he would not answer either of the boys' questions. The next day, as they approached his camp, the same thing happened. His arm was moving back and forth and smoke was pouring out. But again, to Tom and Rick's great frustration, as they approached they could only glimpse at Grandfather's fire kit for a second before he stuffed it into his bag. Again he refused to answer their questions.

Tom said that he and Rick discussed all kinds of ideas about how and what Grandfather was doing to create the smoke. Listening to Tom relate the story, it was evident that, at that tender age, his whole life depended on finding out how Grandfather was making fire. They were so tantalizingly close to the secret.

The next day, as soon as they reached camp, he and Rick were sprinting as fast as their lungs and legs would carry them to make sure Grandfather would not hide the kit from them for another agonizing day. This time they weren't disappointed. Grandfather placed the fire-making kit on the ground and walked away from it, leaving the two boys to etch it forever into their minds. "What type of wood did you make the fire kit out of?" they asked Grandfather, frantic to replicate the skill for themselves. "Green oak," came the reply. So they sped off into the woods, found some green oak, and began to copy the working kit as best they could. Now, if you have ever tried making fire the way Grandfather did, using friction to generate heat, you will no doubt sympathize with Tom and Rick at this point. Not only is the technique itself relatively challenging, but it was made almost impossible by Grandfather's instructions to use "green" wood. Tom said as he related the story that for a few weeks he and Rick carved ever improving versions of Grandfather's kit until they were near identical to their mentor's. Then came improving their technique, all the while still unknowingly facing an almost impossible task using green wood. At last, understandably exasperated because in their minds they had copied Grandfather exactly, they went to him and asked why his kit worked and theirs didn't. This time, Grandfather told them to find and use dead, dry cedar. Needless to say, they started a fire almost instantly. From then on, they never looked back. Soon, despite their young age, they were master fire makers.

Grandfather did not give the boys all the answers straightaway because in his opinion that would prevent them from learning as much as they possibly could. He deliberately withheld important information from Tom and Rick so they would understand for themselves *why* certain things were so vitally important. Without their own struggles they would not be as knowledgeable or skillful as their mentor because they would only have a limited number of the pieces of the puzzle. In teaching in this way, Grandfather led the boys not only to understanding how they were doing certain things, but also why.

What happened in this story? Failure and frustration? Yes, but they were part of the journey to one precious thing: independence. This is something I have never seen in the modern education system, which in fact produces the opposite—dependency. On the surface it seemed that Grandfather did not give the boys the maximum support; instead, at certain times he actually did the unthinkable and gave them the minimum, even going so far as to deliberately make their task more difficult. However, he ensured that he gave them every tool they needed to learn deeply with, the most important ones being passion and a love for learning.

What Is Independence?

Let's now look at an area of huge importance for a child's free and full experience of life: *independence*. This is meant in the largest sense of the word. As simple as the word is, independence means many different things to many different people. In the context of this book, it does not mean that children should take on adult roles in life before they are grown up. I am not suggesting that young people take on adult jobs such as paying bills or filing taxes, for example. In the context of our discussion, independence means children's freedom to make choices with a clear understanding of why they are making them. In other words, creating consciously, with awareness of more than just the needs of the physical self. Our role as adults is to assist and support the understanding process. We can and should explain our most complete understandings of life and help children to recognize the choices that are open to them, but we should not tell them what moves to make. If children fully understand their environment, they will feel empowered to make positive decisions. Who could not feel empowered and inspired if they knew they had a soul that is connected to all things, and that they could not fail at this glorious experience called life? As children grow into adults, they should be capable of independently meeting not only their own physical needs, but also their mental and spiritual needs.

True independence requires three things:

- Freedom to choose *what* is experienced.
- Freedom to choose *how* it is experienced.
- The absence of *fear* in the decision process.

For example, one young adult might choose to experience being peaceful, and will do that by becoming a Buddhist monk. Another may choose the same experience, but decide to do so by becoming a medic in the army. The first two factors, the *what* and *how*, are satisfied. The third requirement for independence is the absence of fear in the decision process. It is difficult to make independent choices when we feel an external factor like fear pressuring us to make a certain decision. This concept of making decisions without fear seems very simple, but is almost unheard of in modern society, largely due to our fear-based educational systems. Without true independence, it is unlikely that children's long-term experiences of love, peace, joy, and purpose will change for the better.

The move toward true independence has to start in the formative years. It is easy for children to become reliant on their teachers or parents, and for a time we must accept that this is inevitable. In children's earliest years they do not have enough experiences to be able to make all their choices for themselves. However, as soon as possible, we must encourage them to develop their own passions, independent of adults and of the education system (whatever form it takes). Otherwise, as soon as either the parent or teacher is removed, learning and exploration are also greatly at risk of vanishing. As we encourage children to become independent, we help to set them on the road to meaningful and enriching long-term experiences.

Why Do We Turn Away From Learning?

If we change our view of what we are doing with our children from "educating" them to providing the opportunity for experiences, there will be no point at which the experiencing stops.

When we say learning, particularly lifelong, we should not confine ourselves to our current narrow definition of education, which is largely based on the memorization of facts and the meeting of external expectations. True independent learning is not necessarily about books or information, but about adventure and seeking new experiences in life.

It is unfortunate that a great number of people stop learning anything new the moment they leave formal education. They have their pieces of paper with various labels (passes, fails, honors, degrees, etc.) on them. Most young adults have in some form earned their ticket into society. For those who stop learning upon leaving formal education, the piece of paper is obviously more important than the knowledge gained. It is certainly more important than the experience. That is to say, the final outcome greatly outweighs the journey. It is understandable that most people are tired after years of academic pressure, testing, stressful learning environments, and fearful experiences. So they choose to get on with life and forget about learning. Perhaps they indulge in a hobby or two, but for the most part their lives of discovery and exploration are over. After all, the system taught them quite clearly that discovery and exploration were merely means to an end. For many young adults, actual learning is all too often reduced to an unfulfilling, hollow, and—now that they have the slips of paper—ultimately pointless experience.

This brings us to the great unanswered question for our society, but particularly for our modern education system: Why do so many children and adults turn away from learning at the first opportunity? When you spend any kind of time with most older children, it is very easy to observe that a true love for life has been lost. The joy of new experiences has been forgotten. A grander purpose has been put aside. It is unfortunate but it is true.

Not for one moment should we believe there is anything natural in this. Nor should we say, "It's a cruel world," or "Life isn't fair," as if adults know about the truth of reality and children do not. There is still a small minority of people who embrace the passion for learning and love for life with which we are all born, well into their adult years. Of course, the way they go about things is not the same as a four-year-old, but the underlying energies of love and joy are there for all to see. We must accept that the current education model is highly successful in turning many children away from long-term learning. In my experience, for those children who turn off, the process is well underway by the time they are just seven or eight years old.

One of the largest and most damaging reasons for both children and adults turning off from learning is that the current system is based almost exclusively on extrinsic rewards. That is to say, the rewards nearly always come from outside the individual, as the result of some external source that measures achievement: passing tests, winning competitions, praise, recognition. And after full-time education, the rewards come in the form of good jobs, money, power, prestige, and career success. But when these extrinsic rewards are taken away, what happens to these "successful learners"? They are no longer learners. It also becomes apparent that they were never independent because the carrot of external success and the stick of external failure were obviously the driving forces of their motivation and their sense of purpose. So we must address both the carrot and the stick.

The carrot of learning simply to achieve external success will only be overcome when we cast aside extrinsic rewards and create an environment where the gains an individual feels from learning are completely internal. These can never be taken away from anyone, and hopefully, as children push themselves to greater things, the internal rewards will stay with them for life. We can do this by encouraging learning simply because it fulfills our innate desire as souls to discover the world, not because it holds fear at arm's length. The soul is the voice that speaks to us in feelings, urging us to experience more. It is the source of our natural desire to learn. As we celebrate and honor not just having a soul but *being* a soul, we will naturally encourage children not only to listen to that voice but also to respond to it. As they do so, children will discover and experience that celebrating their soul is the ultimate reward. They will need nothing outside themselves. In doing this, the external rewards from passing tests will very quickly prove to be worthless in comparison to the sheer joy of listening to and honoring the soul.

The stick of failure can only be overcome by bringing in life's most basic truth: we are all one. If we are only passing tests because without the piece of paper we won't be able to outcompete others, there is likely to be little pleasure taken in the process. But if we know we can't fail, that we can't get thrown to the bottom of the social pile and we won't suffer, fear will have little reason to corrupt our motivation. All this takes to achieve is the simple act of sharing so that everyone may live in dignity. If we truly shared as though we were all one, none of us would have to feel so desperate with our life situation that we would turn to violence or crime against each other. We would not look at another individual or group and feel that their being "winners" made us into "losers". This separation into "haves" and "have-nots" is only possible through exploitation, which inevitably leads to resentment, anger and revenge. The saying, "Live simply so others may simply live" is not just true on a physical, material level, but also on a soul level. By living as if we are all connected in an amazing sea of energy, even our joy for learning is transformed as we honor the fact that all beings have a soul. We and our children will not turn off from learning because we will have returned to our most natural state of desiring to experience life in all its glory and majesty.

TRULY ALIVE TIP ✍ ✍ ✍ ✍ ✍ ✍

Setting Up the Physical and Mental Environment

How we set up the physical and mental environments around children has a great impact on their choices. We can adapt children's environments to make it far more likely that their interests will develop into passions, simply by following one of nature's most basic laws: conservation of energy.

Let's say for example that you are trying to support a child who has just developed an interest in art. When that child, with their new-found interest in art, walks around the house, what do they find? Is there a sketchbook sitting open on the coffee table with colored pencils sitting next to it? Or do they have to gain the attention of a parent to pull down the art materials from the top of a closet? When a child asks to be able to paint do they find it elicits stress in the adults around them? Or are those same adults inspired by the child's desire for creativity and only too eager to support the child's passion? Which scenarios would be more likely to see the child grow in their love for art, and their love for life?

We can ask ourselves if children have to go *against* the flow of the energy that is around them (which is usually created by the choices of adults) or if the physical and mental energy around them flows *with* them, supporting and enabling them toward a grander life experience.

✍ ✍ ✍ ✍ ✍ ✍

Doing Nothing

From discussions with many parents, teachers, and educators, I know that a common fear is that, if given too much freedom, children will choose to do nothing. This is meant in an apathetic, "There's nothing worth doing round here" sense. Perhaps in the very short term that might be true. Children sometimes choose to do nothing because they have been numbed by this current system, and if they get a chance to escape from it, they will. Why wouldn't they? We as adults often try to escape things that bore us. Children are no different.

Another reason children end up doing nothing is that they don't know what else to do. The system is so overwhelming that it leaves little scope for a them to have any creative thoughts. When they don't have someone telling them what to do all the time, they become stuck, unable to act. I have taught a number of children who would not (from fear of failure) or could not use their imagination, especially when they knew they were being assessed. However, given encouragement, support and, most importantly, space and time away from the pressures to perform and succeed, children can and will revert back to their natural state of being curious, using their imagination and being remarkably creative.

TRULY ALIVE TIP 🌿🌿🌿🌿🌿🌿

Responsibility Develops Purpose

Every human needs a true sense of purpose in order to enjoy life fully. As children grow up, we must be careful neither to tell them exactly what their purpose will be, nor diminish their sense of place and belonging. It is not for us to decide what a child's purpose in life is, but it is up to us to help them find it.

So many people complain about the youth of today—that they hang around, cause trouble, have no ambition, and don't contribute anything to society. One of the main reasons for this is that we just don't let them. Depending on the country, we currently say that children are not fit for responsibility and to contribute to society until their eighteenth or twenty-first birthday.

Our youth have so much to offer, so much energy to give to society, and so many outstanding ideas, but we are determined to keep them stifled—as children who must listen but not speak. Giving children responsibility is not about turning them into twelve-year-old adults, but about allowing them to make meaningful, age-appropriate contributions to the world around them.

We should encourage children to strengthen their sense of purpose whenever possible. Among other things, it helps them to become independent, and to create their own path in life. At the center of this support is increasing their responsibility, to which children always seem to respond well. When I was an elementary school teacher, the first thing I would do with a child who had behavior issues was give them responsibility. No matter how small the task, this never failed to bring about some degree of positive response from the child.

Ideally, purpose should be encouraged by helping the child to become responsible for life. This could be directly, such as taking care of a plant, a patch of ground, a pet, or even a sibling, or indirectly, by helping others to support their own lives, such as helping to cook a meal that will benefit the whole family.

Children who grow up in this manner will experience that they are part of the ebb and flow of life—learning and sharing knowledge and wisdom, giving support and being supported. They come to understand that they can take care of themselves because they can take care of others. They know they are never alone, something that is far too rare among children in our current society. Most importantly, they experience that they have a place and purpose that is not forced upon them by the adult world.

꧁꧂꧁꧂꧁꧂

Celebrating Struggles

It is important to consider what to some might seem an absurd idea: we should, at carefully chosen times, just like Grandfather in the fire-making story, give children only the *minimum* support necessary for their success. To understand this, ask yourself what would happen to a baby if, every time she tried to exercise her leg muscles to stand, someone picked her up? In the long term, it is entirely possible the baby would not learn to walk. Or what would happen if, every time a child tried to tie his shoelaces, someone ran over and tied them for him? The child would never learn to tie them for himself. What would happen if, every time children struggled with something in their lives, we did the task for them, to save them from the pain? This occurs on all levels, body, mind and soul, but is particularly prevalent in our minds. Most of our judgments as to whether something causes us discomfort are put forward by the small mind—the mind of separation and fear. It screams at us to turn away from certain experiences because in the past, due to our lack of understanding of who we really are, we have caused ourselves to suffer. Most of the time we are actually suffering very little physically, and our souls are most certainly not experiencing pain. Our eternal life-force is undamaged by anything we can throw at it, however horrific or traumatic it may seem.

One child I worked with on a fire-making program, Kam, highlights for us the importance of understanding that shielding children from their pain, struggles, and hardship provides little opportunity for personal growth; in fact it can have the opposite effect. Kam spent two whole days shrinking his world so he would not have to experience any kind of pain or discomfort. As soon as the onus was on him to try making fire for himself, he immediately declared it was impossible, despite the fact that he had seen it work just two minutes before. He refused to work independently, demanding that the adults help him because, as he stated, "I won't be able to do it by myself." He was absolutely convinced that it would be emotionally traumatic for him.

The most heart-rending piece of this experience for me was feeling the fear and pain in his voice and in his actions. He lurched from sitting motionless to outbursts of anger and then to the verge of tears, all because he did not want to experience pain in any way. In this case the hardship would take the form of small failures along the way that would allow him to learn, progress and expand his abilities. This fire-making was not a test. There were no external prizes for success and no repercussions for failure. All the children were there because they wanted to learn. Kam just could not cope with any kind of setback or struggle. He was obviously used to getting everything he wanted first time, with minimum effort. When he finally agreed to help himself (after he saw other children were not only in no way breaking down, but actually loving the journey) we gave him support. Kam ultimately succeeded in producing a fire, something he was still proclaiming to be impossible two minutes before it happened.

I don't know if Kam enjoyed any part of that two-day program. He spent the whole time convincing himself of his own limits and the limits of life to justify his withdrawal into a smaller world. Kam is like millions of other children who are suffering immensely because we have created a cotton-wool society. We attempt to save children from experiencing any kind of discomfort, but in doing so we create an environment in which they suffer constantly, fearing that at any moment pain will strike. Our attempts to improve their lives by providing a constant sense of safety, security and comfort has rendered our children a shadow of their true potential selves. Thomas Merton, an American Trappist Monk, summed it up beautifully when he said, "The truth that many people never understand, until it is too late, is that the more you try to avoid suffering the more you suffer because smaller and more insignificant things begin to torture you in proportion to your fear of being hurt."

The times we are truly alive are when we grow—when we experience a grander reality. Our views on pain have become distorted because as adults we refuse to make friends with it. We have devised too many ways to look in a different direction. Young children play a game where they think that if they can't see you, you can't see them. This is the game we are playing with any kind of perceived hardship, but it does not end in laughter, it ends in misunderstanding, withdrawing from the truth of who we really are, and above all, it ends in suffering.

Suffering is a miraculous teacher. It shows us where our misunderstandings are, where we can heal our false ideas about ourselves and our connection to life. Think back to something in your life that at the time was painful for you. I am almost certain you can think of something positive you learned from the experience.

For many of us, the death of a loved one is a source of great suffering in our own experience. We create huge blocks in our energy systems, thereby greatly restricting our connection to the eternal and loving nature of life.

When I was in my late teens my mother developed breast cancer that eventually spread to her whole body, and she left this world. Understandably, given our current mainstream teachings around death, I saw this as a terrible thing that had happened to me. What a loss. What a tragedy. My own sense of being a victim, of having suffering inflicted upon me, was reinforced by the people around me who were extremely well meaning but who were obviously carrying their own pain around, caused by similar experiences in their own lives. I sank lower and lower, feeding my suffering through my refusal to confront it and to understand what life was actually telling me. I had my beliefs and I was sticking to them, no matter how much they caused me to close off from life. It took me to hit my own personal rock bottom before I decided to confront those beliefs and sift through them to discern truth, (which always heals) from illusion (which so often causes more pain).

I finished work one day around lunchtime, drove home, picked up a bottle of whiskey, headed down to my bedroom in the basement and numbed myself to my pain. It wasn't long before I had given myself the illusion of escaping my "terrible life." Then I had a sense of leaving my own body (I knew this was independent of and not caused by the alcohol—it was too real), moving to the edge of the room and turning round to look at myself, lying on the floor. At the time I had no idea where the feeling came from, but I remember distinctly understanding on a very deep level that *I had simply to make a different choice. To understand who I really was.* Then I passed out.

The next few years I searched for a different choice to make and the strength to make it. I searched for who I really was, and it was the answer to this which provided the doorway to healing. The journey was, and remains, an incredible experience. I went out and listened to what life was actually telling me about death. I refused to remain the victim, and I refused to accept other people's ideas of how we should relate to life.

Life did not let me down—exactly the opposite. By exploring every last nuance of what I understood to be death, I was lifted up from being passed out on a basement floor to being exhilarated and inspired every day. Where before I saw loss and cruelty, I now see life and love. Great suffering was transformed into even greater healing. Misunderstanding was transformed into deep knowing. Withdrawal was transformed into opening up to the greatest gift that life can offer: understanding and experiencing *who I really am.* I know that I am not finished with my healing—the journey is long—but it is a journey that is a most welcome one.

In no way do painful experiences have to remain as emotional baggage, weighing us down and blocking our experience of being truly alive. Our greatest source of suffering can always be, over time, transformed into our greatest friend. Indeed it must if we and our children are to truly experience love, peace, joy, and purpose.

Suffering, when viewed for what it really is, becomes the catalyst for truly remarkable transformation. If we want our children to experience lives of love, peace, joy, and purpose we must ensure that they have the tools to transform their own suffering into the most wonderful gift life has ever given them. This can only stem from ourselves as adults finding the strength to do so in our own lives, and passing this on to the next generation. Otherwise how are children to heal themselves? How are they to re-connect with the eternal nature of who they really are? How are they to be truly alive?

We are doing our children a huge disservice by constantly shielding them from experiencing pain, and struggling for their so-called successes. In the long term we are simply creating an environment where children are paralyzed, unable to escape the prisons of their own making.

To create a culture where we celebrate suffering as a teacher and as a friend means understanding deeply who we really are. Experiencing pain and struggling to succeed does not mean we are failing; it means we are doing exactly what our souls intend for us to do: experience life to its fullest. It is inevitable that at some points along the journey we will come up against things that are so far outside our comfort zone we will cause ourselves to close down and experience fear and pain. Yet this should simply highlight an area of life we can expand and create a greater reality around. At first our experience may push us beyond our comfort zone, and we can experience fear and great pain. If in time we do not come back to this pain and seek to heal it there is no doubt we will create a huge "no-go" area in our lives.

When children are willing to embrace their suffering, to look it in the eye and ask the simple question, *what is this teaching me?* they will find that the situation inevitably loses its painful sting. Even more than this, by taking this approach, we can begin to see our struggles as a friend—a sure sign we understand who we really are. No child should ever think that the way things are now is how they always have to be, or that they do not have the power to change their experience. We must give children the understanding that they have no limits, they are never confined. Each of us is a being of unlimited creativity; we have no bounds, now or ever. We are part of life and life is part of us. Suffering simply shows us where we have reached a limit, and as Malcolm Ringwalt of the Earth-Heart Institute says, "When we encounter a limit we can know it is false." Pain of this nature can indeed be celebrated, for it points to another false limit we can leave behind. In doing so, our children become truly alive because there is nothing that prevents them from experiencing life fully and freely, from rejoicing for all to see, safe in the knowledge of who they really are.

Accepting "Mistakes"

A common thread runs through the experiences of many adults who are highly skilled at what they do. They made, and still make, many mistakes, but they have a different perception of what most would describe as "failure." They understand that a mistake is not failure at all but all part of a glorious experience. The fear of failure seems to leave those individuals who experience that they are a soul, connected to all things. They know that, even if they make mistakes, both they and others—and the whole of life—will be absolutely fine.

There is a famous story of what happened just before Thomas Edison invented a practical, working light bulb. When asked how he felt about his repeated failures, apparently he replied, "I have not failed. I've just found 10,000 ways that won't work."

Just like Tom and Rick in our earlier story, I lost count of the number of times I failed to make fire by friction before my first success. I messed up every possible aspect of it. But each time I failed, I asked myself, why? What stopped this from working?" Slowly but surely my mistakes diminished until one day, after many hours of blood, sweat, and tears, I managed to do it. I value the learning of that skill above all others, not because it is better than other things I have learned, but because it showed me that the journey is what makes us strong, what teaches us, and what allows us to follow a path to mastery. When I now teach this skill to others, the people I see who are the most accomplished are those who go wrong but do not give in at the first sign of mental or emotional discomfort. They understand that everything is a journey, and that things that are really worth pursuing, that speak to us on a soul level, will rarely come to us instantaneously.

Independence means so much more than just young adults providing for their own physical needs. All children must feel empowered to make their own decisions, to determine how they will experience life. Most crucially this process must take place in the absence of fear. This is one of our greatest challenges. Taking a step back from children's lives in order to improve them is not something we normally see advocated. It goes against so much that we ourselves were taught. Yet if we have brought wisdom to a child's life, they will be able gradually to develop independence over a number of years. It will not just magically arrive when they reach an arbitrary age. True independence is not measured in time, but in wisdom—physical, mental and spiritual.

As individuals and as a society, we must find the strength and courage to give children the gift of *independence*. We can give this gift by choosing to do so.

CHAPTER 10

Questions and Answers Support Independence

No man really becomes a fool until he stops asking questions.

~Charles Steinmetz

Just One Question

One summer my wife, Kat, and I had travelled out to the Western slopes of the Rocky Mountains to offer some nature reconnection programs and found ourselves with a day and a half off. There was no question about what we would do. We looked on a map for anything marked "wilderness" and made a beeline for it. The journey would be relatively brief, but we didn't mind. We knew better than to judge the quality of an experience by how long it lasted.

We left our car at the end of a rutted five-mile road. It was very early in the morning, but already we could tell the weather was going to be kind to us. The sun was just rising over the mountains east of us with not a cloud in the sky to impede its rays. We stepped through the gate that marked off our civilized world from the wilderness beyond and found ourselves in a pristine wildflower meadow. Every color in the rainbow was represented, each stem, leaf and petal reaching proudly for the sun. Farther back rose tall aspens that, when the gentle breeze stirred them, seemed to whisper their secrets to anyone who would listen with more than just their ears. Birds flitted to and fro, singing and chirping to maintain their territory. The mountains stood majestically in the background, their enduring strength seeming to make them the natural keepers of this land. Below us, the river wound its way through the landscape, providing a haven for beaver, deer, and trout. It looked almost too perfect, like a wondrous Garden of Eden, where everything exists in complete harmony.

Neither of us moved for a long while. In my head, dozens of questions were spinning. Where do the elk move, and what do they eat around here? Where are the mountain lions right now, and will we see some sign of them? What plants around here are edible? What are the birds telling us is happening in their world at this moment? I enjoyed the feeling of being overwhelmed with questions. It was like standing before the world's most sumptuous banquet and being allowed to choose whatever you want. You can't possibly try everything all at once, but you know whatever you try is going to send you into into ecstasy.

We spent some time identifying unknown plants, exploring them with all our senses, smelling their fragrance, feeling their leaves and tasting the ones that were edible. We continued walking, heading along a well-worn trail before turning off into the trackless wilds. We didn't intend going far in just a day and a half, but getting off that human path was like stepping into a different world. I could feel my soul reveling in the feeling of freedom, thanking me profusely.

When we searched for a place to make a simple shelter for the night, we asked the Earth for guidance, and then paid attention to the messages that came back. We received a quick, definite answer. A tiny, iridescent green hummingbird shot out of nowhere and flitted between Kat and me, just inches from our eyes. After more agitated movements, all designed to tell us to back off, the hummingbird settled down. Looking around, we found it sitting on a nest. We knew we wouldn't stay, but we took a few moments to try to etch that scene into our memory. The nest, so delicate, the size of a thimble and held together with spider webs, and the tiny birds upon it, were so magical they looked as though they could have been designed by a forest fairy. We headed on and made camp elsewhere.

The next morning, we awoke to another day in paradise filled with encounters with porcupine, grouse, snakes, and fish. We delighted in the trees, mountain streams, animal tracks, and much more. If there are places more awe-inspiring in the world I have yet to see them. When it was time to head back for an evening work appointment, neither of us was the least bit upset. Our souls had been filled to the brim by that beautiful valley and we knew we'd return one day.

We found the human trail again and were about an hour away from the parking lot when we encountered a couple in their late fifties, rushing in the opposite direction. By their speed, I half thought at first there was an emergency up the trail and foolishly asked if everything was okay. Too late, I remembered that's how most people walk, in a mad dash between point A and point B. I felt silly when they stopped, looked at me a little strangely, then smiled and said hello. We chatted for a few minutes, mainly with the woman. The man was quieter and seemed almost agitated. After a little more small talk about the glorious weather and where we were from, the man asked a question

I don't think I will ever forget. He nodded in the direction of the trail and said, "Is there anything worth seeing up there?" I laughed, because I thought he was making a joke. But he was deadly serious, and what's more, he was waiting for an answer. I stammered, but nothing formed into words. I looked around at the Garden of Eden we were standing in, trying to find some Hollywood-esque feature that might be worthy of his attention. "There's a river," I said, half in answer, half in question. "Thanks," he replied, and with that they were off as though they were late for the last train home.

In an environment that looked as though the gods themselves had got together to create a heaven on Earth, in a place where every step you took you could ask a hundred different questions that would lead to as many different adventures, in a place where a dozen lifetimes wouldn't be enough to discover all the secrets it held, his question was, "Is there anything worth seeing up there?"

As we headed home, I could not get that man and his question out my head. If truth be told, I could hear my own voice ten years earlier in his words, and I could guess at what was going to happen. One day, it was very likely that this man would realize all that he had missed in life. It was just a matter of time. Would it be later that day that the absurdity of his question dawned on him, or would he realize with his last breath that we live every day in heaven if we would just awaken to it?

I remember my own day of becoming aware of this, an awakening even, and it was not a pretty experience. It is a huge understatement to say I was upset with myself for having wasted years of my life, eyes closed and ears shut, deaf to the beauty all around me. I vowed from then on that I would go on adventures every day and ask a hundred questions if that's what it took to find a single answer. Yet, above all, I would remember that it is not the answers that bring us to life, it's the questions we ask.

Asking Questions

What are the other means by which we can bring about independence for children? The first is one that relates most strongly to purpose. It is the means by which children will come to know themselves and the world around them. Simply, it is the ability and desire to ask questions. We must make a positive, conscious effort to encourage children to ask questions about all aspects of life—deep, far-reaching questions that are asked with passion. Our role as facilitators must be to support this process. But, just as importantly, adults must give children genuine space in which to question freely and fully.

It is vital that we as facilitators discard the idea that children must form a certain opinion. This idea stems from our own fears and misunderstandings about life. The current system has limitations because it dictates that there must always be a result, a conclusion, a very specific destination in mind. Because the teacher is usually trying to get the child to attain a narrow, predefined outcome, the child is encouraged to question, but continually steered toward meeting the set curriculum and passing the prescribed tests. In other words, they are always guided toward asking the "right" questions to obtain the "right" answers. Clearly, this is not independence, and it does not lead to an enriched life.

We have to let go of our expectations and our fears and accept that children may ask questions and form opinions that are different from our own. They may choose to lead different lives. This is okay. If children do not reach the same conclusions as we do, it doesn't mean that we have failed or that we are wrong. We each do the very best we can with our children, given our view of the world. Now we have to ask ourselves, can we find the strength to encourage children to reach for something greater, to aspire to something grander? Can we support children in experiencing lives of love, peace, joy, and purpose *on their own terms* regardless of the changes this may bring in our own lives?

The Questions Themselves

There is power in simplicity. We often lead ourselves away from truth by believing that questions and answers should be as complex as possible. Usually, however, the opposite is true. Simple questions, when answered honestly, lead to great truths. In a child's process of gaining independence, two questions should be constantly asked by both facilitator and child alike. They ensure that we are living our own truth and not that of others. They are:

- What happened here?
- What does this mean to me?

Life has no meaning except that which we give it. Far too many of us, billions in fact, allow others to dictate to us what something means to us in our lives. It is little wonder that the real problems of humanity—war, famine, poverty, and depression, to name but a few—have never been truly addressed. We have allowed ourselves to stop asking our own questions, which are vital to our living freely and fully. What does love mean to me? What do peace and joy mean to me? Who am I, why am I here, and what purpose do I choose? Instead, we have allowed others to inform us of how life is, and what we should be concerned with. Because we have stopped asking our own questions and discovering our own truths, we have allowed others to shape our lives for us. We have become reduced to being obsessed with competing against everyone and everything for our own survival. Yet we could save ourselves a great deal of pain and suffering by returning to asking our own questions and deciding on our own answers.

The search for answers will be a gift of exploration and unlimited potential. It will truly be a gift of love and freedom.

What happened here? What does this mean to me? These are the questions that will bring purpose to our children's lives. Love, peace, and joy will follow as children greatly expand their experience of who they are, because their experiences will quickly lead them to the soul, and a connection with all things. After that, there are no limits. Children will reach the understanding that they have unlimited potential and are not confined to the small worlds that others would have them believe they are bound to. They do not need to fight to get ahead of others to survive. They will learn that their soul cannot be hurt or die, because it is life itself, it is part of the Oneness and will always be so. These questions will lead to the grandest enquiries and the finest ideas. They will take children far beyond the limited questions and experiences of the fear-based school system. They will, in short, transform children's beliefs and create new ones to bring about a free and full life experience.

TRULY ALIVE TIP 🌿🌿🌿🌿🌿🌿

Telling Stories

Stories can heal, inspire, and educate. They are part of the fabric of human culture. We are surrounded by and are also part of hundreds of different stories every day. Most of us can think of stories that have played a positive role in our lives. Movies, books, religion, songs, family recollections, and even ads and TV commercials all have us captivated through their stories. And we never tire of telling stories about how life came to exist.

We tend to think of adults telling stories to children, but we can switch this around to great effect. Encouraging children to tell stories to adults not only encourages their creativity and imagination, but also offers rich opportunities for facilitators to reinforce and extend learning.

For example, let's take something as seemingly mundane as encouraging a child to tell us the story of her day. As she recalls what happened to her, she is first reinforcing her own learning. For example, let's imagine during a walk in the woods that the girl followed a bird call and found the source of the sound. She might recall and repeat the song and explain the colorful markings on the bird's wings. This ensures that the learning takes place on an even deeper level, because whenever we take the time to explain to someone else, we have to organize our own thoughts. As the child explains her experience with the bird, the imagery in her mind is made much clearer and sharper.

The second aspect of the power of storytelling arises through questioning the storyteller to find out the nuances of the experience. Using the same example, the adult could ask any number of questions about the child's recollection of the bird. How did the bird move? Why did it move? Did it have a nest, or young chicks?

We can group the questions into three different types. First, the majority of the questions should increase the breadth and depth of learning by fostering awareness of what the child already knows. So if the child saw the bird fly but did not describe this as part of her story, the adult could ask her to recall this aspect.

The second group of questions can be thought of as encouraging the child to expand her awareness of the experience, but, in contrast to the first group, these questions may not be things she can directly recall. These questions may stoke her imagination and motivation to return to the experience and learn more. For example, did the bird have a nest? Probably the child cannot answer definitively or immediately, but with a little bit of effort and passion she may realize that she can solve the mystery.

The last type of question should be used sparingly. These can be described as seed-planters. The adult asks a question that will plant a seed that will grow over time and may one day be explored. In our example, the question posed to the child may be, "Was the bird letting you know if there were other animals around?" It should be a question the child didn't even know you could ask, let alone find the answer to. It's possible she will laugh and say that's impossible. But as she enjoys more experiences around birds, the seed question may one day return, and she herself will ask the question and begin to explore it.

Seeking Answers

Teachers are the key factor in handing children the knowledge to pass a test and to be successful in the system. They know what questions will be asked and they know what answers are supposed to be given. They hold the key to the door of the winners' circle. Children most certainly understand this.

After I had been an elementary school teacher for a few years, a child asked me a question regarding the subject the class was working on. I thought for a few moments and then answered simply and honestly, "I don't know." There was silence in the classroom as thirty pairs of eyes swiveled toward me. The children's mouths were agape. One of them said, "But Mr. Harrison, you're a teacher. You're supposed to know *everything*." He was absolutely serious, and his fellow classmates agreed: teachers should know everything. These children were ten years old. They were mature and intelligent, but they were convinced that was how the system worked: teachers knew everything. I was stunned, but explained that no one in the world has all the answers. And when you do get an answer—no matter who from—you should question it to see if it feels right for you. Not surprisingly, this didn't go down well at first. I had shattered some of the children's securities about life. It took most of them a number of hours just to believe

I wasn't joking. In the long term, I saw that some of them visibly benefited from understanding that teachers don't know everything, while others just wanted to be told the facts and weren't really interested in asking questions. Unfortunately, the belief in teachers as oracles is currently very normal for children, and it has far-reaching consequences that are harming much more than just their ability to ask questions.

We see this challenge in schools every day. A child has a question. He knows the teacher must have the answer, so without hesitation he approaches the teacher and asks it. Provided the knowledge is required learning (part of the curriculum), the teacher is only too happy to provide the answer immediately or to respond with one or two simple questions that within seconds the child has "answered." The words "been given" could be substituted for "answered" and the statement would still be accurate.

This means "success" for everyone. The child has an answer to his question. The teacher has helped to move the child one step closer to absorbing the required curriculum. The school will probably achieve better exam results, and the nation's politicians can say that children are better educated because more of them than ever are passing exams.

Yet where is the true success? How are the children actually benefiting? Where is the joy of learning? Where is the child's far-reaching, passionate enquiry? Where is the hands-on experience that leads to wisdom? Most importantly, where is the true success for the child in this method of teaching?

The following outcomes are very likely if the example just given is played out over days, weeks, months, and years:

- Children learn that answers come quickly and easily. Answers in this world do not have multiple layers. That is, they are generally without depth.
- Children come to see the teacher as an "oracle." The teacher

is the external source to whom they take their questions and from whom they get their answers.

- Children have accepted the teacher's word as the truth, instead of seeking their own truth. This may be the worst of all.

A quick answer is not necessarily a bad answer, but it robs children of opportunities to explore and experience the world for themselves and so often slowly erodes natural curiosity. Let's take a look at these all wrapped up into a simple example.

A lucky child is with her class on a field trip in the woods when she comes across something she doesn't recognize. She—being deeply embedded in the educational culture—runs to the teacher and asks, "What kind of tree is this?" The teacher, happy the child is excited about nature replies, "That's an oak tree. It's very old, very beautiful." The girl stares for a few seconds and maybe touches the bark. "Cool, an oak tree." And that is literally the end of the experience. She will remember it forever as the thing that has the label, "oak tree."

What happened here? The child did not even consider for a half second that she should think for herself. She went straight to her source of information, the teacher, and asked the question. But what will happen when the teacher is not there? Will the answers stop? Probably. More importantly, will the questions stop? Unfortunately, the answer is the same—probably.

The problems surrounding this are very much intertwined and ingrained. Teachers are giving the answers because that is what has come to be expected of them by all levels of society, including children, parents, and the education system. But society also (supposedly) wants the child to become independent. We must question whether our current methods do in fact support independence and lifelong learning, or whether we would do well to encourage a greater degree of child-directed, free exploration. This would be a good start, but the issue of raising independent children cannot be addressed in isolation. It is not quite as simple as that. The next layer we have created that causes great difficulty and suffering for everyone is the problem of time. Currently, there is no time to waste on free exploration if our children are to learn all the facts necessary to be "successful." Not once as a regular school teacher did I have enough hours in a day to teach children everything that I should have. There was constant pressure to make sure I was not failing the children by giving them even a few seconds off from learning—and I don't believe for a moment that this has changed since I left mainstream teaching. I couldn't afford to, otherwise, by the end of a school year, there would be entire units of work—government-dictated essential curricula—that there was not enough time for. No wonder recess is being cut, more homework is being given, and children spend their summer vacation being enrolled in even more school. This is heart-rending, because when you spend time with children you can see so clearly and easily that it is slowly killing them. It is killing their passion, their creativity, and it is killing any awareness they have of their soul.

The way we define it right now, success can't just wait around for children in the hope that during their exploration they find the answer that's in the curriculum (the "successful" answer). Instead, children are given answers as quickly and often as possible. An argument could easily be made that this is not true learning.

Giving immediate answers has created its own set of problems. Naturally, as this is repeated over time, children will come to expect the same from life—that answers should be instantaneous. So many young people give up at the first sign of a challenge or are completely distraught at their first experience of failure. This isn't their fault. We have raised them in a culture that shields them from challenges and conditions them to expect immediate answers and rewards, so it is understandable that most children are extremely fearful of failure.

Our society and our educational systems have turned away from long-term experience and embraced short-term, instant gratification.

TRULY ALIVE TIP

Modeling for Children

The way that adults react to or perceive something has a great influence on the way that a child will learn to relate to the world. Let's use a simple example.

Let's imagine I am out with a group of children in the woods and I come across some animal tracks that were made by a deer. This could be the first time that many children will have seen them. My reaction has a huge influence on those children. If I walk past, point a finger, mutter something about deer tracks, and keep on walking, what have I just communicated? That deer tracks are not something to get excited about, and not worthy of our attention. Conversely, if I am genuinely interested in them and crouch down, start looking at them from a few different angles, and try to work out where the next one is, the chances are that most of the children will follow my example. Now, not every one of those children will grow up to share my passion for deer tracks, but that desire to find out about life around me will undoubtedly be felt, shared, and remembered by everyone present. The children will apply this passion from adults to their own life experiences. What and how we model for children is amazingly powerful. We are all teachers, all the time.

More Questions Than Answers

In our earlier example, the short-term answer of "It's an oak tree" obviously means the child's knowledge has increased, albeit slightly. But consider a different approach for a moment. Imagine the teacher replied not with an answer but with another question. "What does its bark feel like?" Or "What shape are its leaves? What does it smell like? Who lives in its branches?" Now the facilitator is opening doors and instantly adding depth to the query. But, more importantly, they are encouraging personal experience that leads to wisdom. The question, "Who lives in its branches?" might take a lifetime to be answered. When asking these questions, a teacher should be prepared to give a child the time and the opportunity to explore the possibilities—as much as is needed. The child's expectation should be that the onus is on them to find out answers. But the crux of this point is that the child will *want* to find answers more than anything because a genuine love of learning has been nurtured from an early age.

The final layer of challenge we have is to encourage children not necessarily to accept the teacher's answer as the truth. We will look at this in the next chapter. Suffice to say that there should never be a substitute for personal truth through experience. All children should be encouraged to discover, on their own, what is right for them. They can do this through constantly returning to the two-part question, *what is happening here?* and *what does this mean to me?*

Using our oak tree example, here are just a few questions to get you started. Is the oak tree alive? In what way? Does it bear fruit I can eat? Can I communicate with it? In relation to it, who am I? Do I want to write poetry about it, or work out the ratio of roots to branches? Or maybe just sit and relax and make friends with it? There are an infinite number of questions that can only be answered by the individual, based on what each question means to them and who they choose to be. The day we allow other people to answer these questions for us is a sad day indeed.

As facilitators, we should try never to simply give an answer away. If a child wants to know something, an adult can nurture and support that need for knowledge and grow it into something more. We could just scatter seeds on the ground, and some of them might grow. But there is a far greater chance of success if we take the time to plant each seed gently into well-prepared soil, and nourish it with sunlight and water. We can nurture children's passions in the same way by investing even a small amount of time and effort. To do so, one of three things should happen when a child asks a question:

- The correct answer is given, but another question is then posed by the facilitator.
- The answer "I don't know" is given, and the adult suggests to the child, "Why don't we find out the answer together?"
- The question is met with another question.

The response given by the facilitator will depend completely on the child and the situation. Different personalities respond differently to each approach. The most successful responses are usually the first two, but that normally has more to do with the current system than a child's natural state. They generally find it frustrating not to receive some kind of instant answer. After all, they have been conditioned that way. How many children do you know who would not be frustrated if instead of an answer, you gave them a question?

It is human nature to want to learn, to ask questions and to seek answers. This desire would be restored—for the long term and often relatively quickly. We see this time and again when children are released from the pressures and expectations that adults place on them. Children soon return to seeking out what inspires them, rejoicing in their new-found freedom and sense of adventure. Very soon, the child is an independent learner and a lover of life again.

As individuals and as a society, we must find the strength and courage to give the gift of allowing children to *seek answers to the deepest questions*. We can give this gift by choosing to do so.

CHAPTER 11

Finding Truth

Every truth passes through three stages before it is recognized.
In the first, it is ridiculed, in the second it is opposed, in the
third it is regarded as self-evident.

~Arthur Schopenhauer

Children Find Their Own Truths

A great challenge we have with the modern-day education system is that it often struggles to inspire new and creative thinking. Because our measuring system decides the answers ahead of time, it is up to individual children to move their understanding of life in line with the system's. Children *receive* "truth," rather than discovering real truth for themselves. We must look at our beliefs and ask if we have allowed someone else to shape our lives. We must also consider deeply if we are dictating our own truths to children, thereby shaping their lives in the same mould as our own.

TRULY ALIVE TIP 🌿🌿🌿🌿🌿🌿

Soft-Focus

An amazingly effective technique to create a doorway into a larger world is *soft-focus*. This is a different way of using our eyes, and is very complementary to fox walking. It helps to create a very meditative state, which is naturally conducive to being peaceful. As the name suggests, we use more of our vision, and in a different way, enabling us to see life more clearly. But this is not just because we see more of what is going on in the physical world. Spending time in soft-focus vision helps us to see into our soul and to experience with greater clarity our connection to all things.

So how do we go about using soft-focus? It's very simple. There are really only two ways we can use our eyes: we can look at something and go into tunnel vision, or we can take in everything. That's soft-focus. Our field of vision is quite a bit larger than most people think. We want to extend it to every boundary possible. It's quite a bit larger than most people think, and in this exercise we want our vision to extend to every boundary possible.

To move your vision into soft-focus, stand some place where you can stretch your arms out. Then look gently into the distance. For the purposes of establishing your field of vision, keep your head and eyes still—do not move them from side to side. Relax your eyes and let them rest gently on something stationary. Now raise your arms in front of you, outstretched, level with your eyes. Begin to wiggle your fingers. Slowly spread your arms outward as you keep wiggling your fingers. At some point as your arms move out to your sides, you are going to lose sight of your wiggling fingers. Bring your arms back in just to the point where you can see the movement. You won't see the details of your fingers, but you should be aware they are moving. Then repeat the process for up and down. Move one arm down and one arm up until you can only just see the movement of your fingers. This is the extent of your vision with your eyes.

Now, you can't very well go around wiggling your fingers in the air to establish your soft-focus vision every time you want to enjoy its benefits. So take note of the feeling of your eyes and the feeling of your body. Make a conscious choice to go into tunnel vision. Look at something in particular for a few seconds, and then return to that feeling of soft-focus vision. With even a short amount of practice, you'll find that you can switch effortlessly from one to the other. It's so easy and simple that at any point during the day when you find either you or your children need a little meditative time, this is a great vehicle to achieve it. This is a great way to let go of our doing world and spend time enjoying with that peaceful, connected side of our being

This can be taken to a completely new level if you can invent, or better still encourage children to create, a game that utilizes wide-angle vision as a key skill.

For a powerful peaceful experience, and to experience a world of connections, try combining fox walking and soft-focus vision.

✿✿✿✿✿✿

History Is on Our Side

People who have brought great inspiration to the world have disregarded many of the "truths" that society held at the time. History is littered with examples of people who were not willing to accept other people's version of things, but who chose to go out and *experience* what life was telling them. This can take great courage, especially when everyone else is telling us the opposite. Martin Luther King Jr. had "a dream" that black children and white children could play hand in hand. That dream flew in the face of the widely held "truths" of the time, yet can you imagine us going back to those "truths" now? Thank goodness Dr. King did not accept the beliefs of others as truth but instead sought his own. Through his own beliefs, he brought love and peace to millions.

Princess Diana was one of the first high-profile members of society to touch and even hug AIDS victims. The belief she held that these people deserved love and were perfectly safe to touch flew in the face of the widely held "truths" at the time, but can you imagine going back to that so-called truth now? Like Martin Luther King, Princess Diana did not accept the beliefs of others as truth but instead sought her own. She also brought love and peace to millions.

We could fill a whole book with examples of people who found their own truths to be a grander expression of life than the truths that were held by the general population. Many were ridiculed at the time, but they held to their beliefs because that was what their experiences had shown them. You cannot find your own truths without your own experiences; that is why it is so important to encourage children to seek independence. The possibilities of where it might lead are infinite.

Why not encourage this kind of thinking? What do we have to lose except the illusion of control? If we allow our children to go through life content to live *our* truths, they will be forever walking in our shadow, and they will likely perpetuate the cycle with the next generation. We should not be exerting pressure using the fear of failure to get children to think and behave a certain way. All that demonstrates to a child is that the adult world is extremely fearful of change. In most cases, children will also buy into that fear, and very quickly we have a vicious cycle that becomes the norm, and those who seek change are negatively labeled.

Imagine giving a child a canvas upon which they are free to paint whatever masterpiece they choose, but then guiding their hand to make sure their artwork is identical to ours. There is nothing masterful in that.

We can create an environment that supports free thinking and encourages children to question the knowledge and wisdom we hold, but it will take courage, open minds, and our collective will to change. This does not mean it is not possible. We can quite easily support an environment for children that says yes to questions and yes to honoring an individual's truth. But it will mean an end to our obsession with testing children, and an end to homogenized, externally based education. Are we ready to give that up?

When we live our own truths, we are powerful in every good sense of the word. We are powerful because we have experienced them, and because we have experienced them, we have faith in them. This leads us to many things such as contentment, confidence, and inner peace. But most of all it leads us to a life that we consciously create—every day, every moment—a life that is lived with great purpose. We can believe in ourselves. By encouraging children to find their own truths, we hand them the tools of freedom and personal experience to create their own magnificent lives.

As individuals and as a society, we must find the strength and courage to give children the gift of allowing them to *find their own truths*. We can give this gift by choosing to do so.

CHAPTER 12

The New (Old) Role of the Earth

I do not think the measure of a civilization is how tall
its buildings of concrete are, but rather how well its people
have learned to relate to their environments and fellow man.

~Sun Bear of the Chippewa

The Faster We Go...

From the moment I saw my first deer in the forests of Scotland, I was mesmerized. I had travelled up in an Easter break from teaching, eager for adventures. However, I didn't take nearly enough warm clothing, and when the snow came down each day, my choice was to wrap up in my tent and sleeping bag, or head on out and keep warm by walking. I chose the latter. I went walking in the forests around Aviemore, not going anywhere in particular, just following the path wherever it took me.

The cold numbed me to my core, bothering my mind as much as my body. I was certainly fighting it, even though I knew it was a battle my mind would not win. But then I saw them, and strangely, for the next few hours, I completely forgot I was supposed to be cold. There, not one hundred feet to the side of the trail, were three deer—two does and one buck. Even before my mind kicked into gear, I found myself crouching down behind a small bush, staring at the magnificent creatures ahead of me. I watched, captivated by the way their hot breath formed swirling clouds among the snowflakes. They were feeding on the bushes, seemingly unaware of me, so I decided to try and get as close as I possibly could to one. I'd heard stories of people touching deer and now I was in a perfect position to try for the first time. They definitely had not seen me, and there was almost no wind to carry my scent. I hid behind some shrubs, and the ground, covered with a light dusting of snow, was silent under my feet. I half stood, half crouched, trying to work out the best way to move toward them. Finally, concentrating on the ground, I took my first step toward a nearby bush. A sudden *whoosh* caused me to look up sharply, and to my dismay the deer had seen that first movement and taken off. They did what I have watched hundreds of deer do since—they ran a few paces, and then stopped. I took it as an invitation to try again. And again, and again.

For a couple of hours I played at this, or rather the deer played with me. They were supremely aware. After that first step, I don't believe there was a moment in the next few hours they didn't know exactly where I was. Slowly they walked, sniffing, listening, looking, taking in everything around them, seen and unseen. Most of the time I had no idea where they were. I couldn't see through the bushes so I would creep around them, then the deer would run a few yards, and the whole thing would start again.

I was quickly learning that their awareness far outstripped mine—it was in a different universe because they needed it to survive and I didn't. Their world was one of sensing, and I knew that even without smelling, seeing, or hearing me they were well aware of my presence. If you've ever tried to get near enough to touch a deer, you will have no doubt developed a supreme respect for them. In the wild, no deer is going to approach you or even let you get past a critical point. When you cross that threshold, they run because you are a threat to them. Their life depends on their being acutely aware, and their awareness depends on their moving delicately and cautiously, in tune with the Earth that nourishes them.

This was not the end of my lessons from the deer; it seemed they wanted to show me both sides of the coin. I was at a spot where I like to sit near a river by my home in Colorado, in an area with a large deer population. Like all other deer, whether they are in Scotland or America, these deer were extremely aware. On this day, though, one doe had almost entirely sacrificed her awareness, and it could so easily have been the end of her life if she had run into a dangerous place such as the nearby road. I heard thuds in quick succession, which I knew could only be a large animal running through the woods, and by the sound and pattern it was almost certainly a deer. I only had to wait a few seconds to find out. I watched as the doe came charging down one side of the small canyon, splashed through the water, and charged up the other side where I was sitting. I knew I was in full view, certainly not hard to spot for a wild animal, but she continued to hurtle toward me. I still have no idea what made her run like that, but on she came. When she was about thirty feet from me, it occurred to me that she hadn't seen me, but that hardly seemed possible because these creatures seemed the masters of awareness. As the doe raced directly at me, at the last minute I took evasive action, shielding my face with my arms and curling tight into a ball. I could feel the wind created by her body as she galloped past and saw the dirt fly out of the tracks she was making in her blind panic. On she went over a small ridge and out of sight. I don't believe that even inches from me she was ever aware I was there.

What had changed? It was the speed at which the deer was moving. The faster any animal moves, the more awareness it sacrifices and the less it senses of the world around it. Some animals know this. Some don't. Some animals sacrifice their awareness because of a real, immediate threat. Others do so moment to moment, voluntarily. We are no different. As we live our lives at the breakneck pace of society, we have given up a corresponding level of awareness of what is actually going on. The answers to our greatest challenges are right in front of us, but neither adults nor children will find them unless we adopt the wisdom of the slow, highly aware deer, listening and watching with patience, observing what is actually happening, not what we think or wish to be true. Unless we slow down to the pace of the Earth, our lack of awareness will see us continue to hurtle down the same path we have been following for centuries, toward complete destruction of life as we know it.

Nature Connections

We all yearn for connections with the natural world. We go for walks in the park; we take plants into the house and office. This innate desire of humans to be close to nature even has a name, *biophilia*, which in Latin means "a love of life and the living world." Unfortunately, over the last few centuries, our connection with the Earth has been greatly diluted. We spend almost all our time in environments that are artificially controlled, shielded from the outside world. How often do we know which way the wind is blowing or what the birds are saying? We buy food from a store in neat, clean packages. Where does it come from? Who knows what is healthy to eat nowadays? Most of our knowledge of the natural world comes from television, print media, and the Internet. It is second- or third-hand information. We do not understand, at a fundamental level, the very life that sustains us. Wisdom has receded as our lives have become increasingly removed from the natural world. This is because we have turned away from our greatest teacher, the Earth. Most cultures in the world are now so far removed from the Earth that it is seriously damaging the health of society, the individuals in it, and also the planet itself.

Mother Nature is a remarkable teacher. She is subtle, powerful, patient, and loving. If a child asked me to explain how to be loving, I would lead them to the Earth. If they asked me for insight into how to be wise, I would do the same. The Earth speaks to us, communicates, and teaches us on an entirely different level from that which we're used to, especially within the confines of our schools and other institutions, separated from the outside world. As we spend time in nature, every part of our being is affected. The connection goes so deep it seems to affect our very core, or—to use a different word—our *soul*. The Earth brings light to our lives in ways scientists are just beginning to explain.

This connection to nature has untold benefits. We cannot be fully alive if we place ourselves in environments that are stagnant—that is, indoors. Time spent in nature recharges our souls, because at some level we can feel the connection we have to all living things. We plug ourselves back in to life as we are part of the flow once again. The Earth sustains us in more ways than most of us ever think about. Only now, with humanity's devastating effects on the planet, are we even slightly beginning to understand the folly of removing ourselves from the source of our natural lives.

If we are successful in leading our children to a place where they can experience love, peace, joy, and purpose, it will be because we have guided them to the Earth. Then we must step out of the way and allow children to form their own relationships with nature, without us as a go-between. In this we again cease to be teachers and become facilitators and supporters. We can facilitate children reconnecting with the Earth. We can allow them to commune with nature and discover that they are more than they have ever dreamed.

Just the health benefits of being outside are worthy of many books by themselves. In this book, we are predominantly concerned with children's experience of life. The Earth is central to this for many reasons, but one stands out in particular. A real connection with the natural world will allow children personally to experience at least three of the greatest gifts that are available to us:

- Connection with all of life.
- Living in the present.
- Finding our own truths.

Every single one of us has a connection to the Earth, but for most it has become weak and distorted. It has been discarded in favor of what Tom Brown Jr. describes as "false gods of the flesh." As adults, we know that a life spent doing only things that please the body leaves us with precious little fulfillment. Moreover, a life spent worshipping consumerism—always craving something bigger, better, faster, and more—is undoubtedly a hollow one. Can we support children in re-awakening their relationship with the Earth? Can we encourage them to leave behind these "false gods of the flesh?" Can we lead them instead to the life-giving experiences of a true connection with the Earth?

The connection is still relatively strong in children but every day we force them further away from a place of great love. We steer them away from their grandest joy and their greatest potential. The time is long overdue for this pattern be reversed. New lives and a new education paradigm can be built with a deep connection to the Earth at its very center. I have seen children transformed by even a couple of hours spent truly connected to the Earth, to say nothing of days, weeks, months and years.

It needs to be emphasized that being outdoors is not necessarily the same as actually experiencing a connection with the Earth. A suitable analogy would be the difference between being on a boat looking down into a deep blue ocean, or actually jumping in. The latter would mean experiencing the ocean with all our senses, our whole being. We would be quite literally immersed in it. The same goes for being outdoors. We don't just want children to scratch the surface of the wonders of nature; we want their whole being—body, mind, and soul—to be immersed in it.

There is no prescription for an exact way to reconnect children with the Earth. It will naturally be different for us all. If you are wondering how to enable this experience for your children, a good place to start is to follow their passions. What interests them? Where are they telling you they want to reconnect? Maybe it's growing their own food, or painting a landscape. It could be hiking in the mountains, or making a natural shelter in the woods. However you can give this gift, make it a personal experience for children. Through personal experience comes a deep, personal connection. A life lived close to the Earth will undoubtedly find an abundance of love, peace, joy, and purpose.

Earth-Time

An integral part of reconnecting children with the natural world will be the movement toward *Earth-time*. This is consciously living with the flow of the natural world, moving in harmony with the rhythms of the Earth. It certainly means slowing down our physical lives, but it is so much more than that. Earth-time means plugging ourselves back in with the life-force that surrounds us all, listening to its nuances, and understanding what it is communicating to us. It means letting go of much of our desire to impose our will on all things, and allowing ourselves to be guided to all that we need.

We must recognize that some kind of connection to the Earth

is crucial for the well-being of each individual. We cannot possibly reach our potential stuck inside four walls every day. Also, for the long-term prosperity of all life on this planet, we must each have a meaningful, personal relationship with the natural world. Chief Dan George of the Tsuleil-Waututh Nation said, "What we don't understand we fear, and what we fear we destroy." As our modes of living have moved progressively further away from the Earth, we have become increasingly fearful. In doing so, we have predictably become ever more destructive. We feel that we must conquer and tame nature. We see everything as a resource, to be used for our benefit, to provide personal convenience, to speed up our lives and to outcompete others.

Earth-time is little understood in our culture. We do not currently make a choice to have it in our lives. It does not help people "get ahead," or make them more economically competitive. It does not give us the instant gratification of the body that we crave. And it does not even begin to fill our materialistic desires for bigger, better, faster, and more. There is currently no place for Earth-time in society, and thus we are finding that there is no place for us with the Earth. We are running too fast to see her. We are creating too many distractions to hear her. The very nature of our relationship with the Earth has changed. "She" has become an "it." A living being has become just a "thing" to us.

We will never develop a true connection with nature while we live at the breakneck pace of modern society. We may be able to appreciate some of the beauty, but we will not enjoy a deep, meaningful relationship.

Earth-time is the first step in moving toward creating a more positive relationship with all living things, not only the Earth. At first, it will look as though we are simply slowing down. But more is happening—seeds are being planted. They are growing strong roots and getting ready to flourish. Unlike our demands of life, things connected with the Earth are not instantaneous. This is the first part of what will prove to be a remarkably powerful and life-changing experience for our children's education. So, what benefits can Earth-time bring?

As we spend time in nature, we become more aware on a number of levels. Our sensitivity and understanding of life are increased simply because we feel life happening all around us. We become aware of being part of the flow again. We are no longer cut off. Our bodies change. Physically, we are more sensitive to the nuances both of ourselves and the world around us. At first this is simply because we have slowed down enough to be able to observe. Imagine trying to watch an entire movie in fast-forward mode. It would probably drive you crazy. If you slow it down, however, you may actually get a sense of what's going on, and then life will start revealing itself. Your senses are strengthened and actually experienced as never before. You can see more, hear more, feel more, and even understand more. A whole new world is opened up to you.

Slowing life down to Earth-time, the mind has a chance to still itself. This alone is life-changing. Most of us live in a world that constantly bombards our minds, filling them with images, sounds, and thoughts that do not in any way encourage adults or children to be loving or peaceful, joyful or purposeful. Modern society has us completely distracted from who we really are. It is unlikely that true peace for any of us, especially children, will be easily attainable until we create the opportunity to leave this discordant racket behind. When we do, clarity of thought will return and we will be able to make sense of things; we will see things for what they really are. We will experience the emergence of our old friend, the soul.

Free from distractions, the soul will become something we can physically feel and enjoy, not merely an abstract concept in our minds. It will play a meaningful role in our lives, enriching them beyond all imagination. And, once the genie is out of the bottle, there's no putting it back. As all these experiences happen, we not only conceive of a greater reality, but also actually live it.

As our soul emerges, we will begin to realize that this increased sensitivity and awareness is not impossible to achieve in today's hustle-and-bustle society. Yet it is exceedingly difficult: there is precious little opportunity for children (or adults) to find the kind of peace that is the doorway to deep and meaningful experiences. The differences between Earth-time and the hustle-and-bustle world are immense. Trying to be loving and peaceful in the midst of the distractions of modern society is like trying to walk in a hurricane. It is certainly not impossible, but it takes constant, extraordinary effort.

On the other hand, being peaceful and loving in Earth-time is like gently floating downstream. It supports and enhances our natural states of peace and love, guiding us to experience positive lives that flow with ease and with freedom.

We have to make a conscious choice to allow Earth-time into our lives and into the lives of children; the change will not just miraculously happen by itself. In terms of education, this change will shift the focus from quantity to quality. It shifts from prescription to creation, from fear to love. It changes our world from a two-dimensional gray scale to three-dimensional technicolor. The difference is dramatic.

Earth-time is the basic environment and state of being we should be encouraging if we truly want to facilitate experiences of love, peace, joy, and purpose for children.

TRULY ALIVE TIP 🌿 🌿 🌿 🌿 🌿 🌿

Talking to the Trees

We all need someone to talk to. We have already addressed how listening to each other can be a very powerful act. On occasions, we may find we still need a non-human to talk to and confide in—something that is never going to judge us and will always be there for us. You may well have heard of people who claim to enjoy health benefits from "tree hugging."

A similar but more powerful activity is tree whispering. We can support children's connection with the natural world and also promote their feelings of peace and purpose by encouraging them to whisper to the trees. They can share not only their problems but their hopes and dreams. Communicating in this way to a favorite old tree helps children to create their lives in a more conscious manner. Telling another being about our problems and plans is a powerful way to organize our thoughts. It solidifies our ideas and helps to bring them into reality.

Some Science About Brain Waves

Here we turn briefly to science for some current understandings about what goes on during Earth-time. Science has identified four basic states of being that relate to the frequency of our brain waves. Imagine a radio with four stations, and you can turn the dial to whichever one you choose. None of the stations is better than the others; they just play different kinds of music. A simple example is that when you're wide awake, you are in a different state of being (tuned to a different station) than when you're fast asleep. Science has labeled these four different states of being beta, alpha, theta, and delta. Beta is the most alert, and this is followed by alpha, then theta, and finally delta, which is usually a deep sleep state.

Given that we are talking about education, which happens in our waking hours, beta and alpha are our first focus. The differences between these two states are startling. Of the two, beta is our usual state, but it is not difficult to put forward the case that it is not our *natural* state. The worst aspects of beta states are associated with promoting fear, anxiety, impulsivity, and even attention deficit hyperactivity disorder (ADHD). It is in this state that addictions are most easily and readily indulged. The majority of people (particularly adults) spend most of their time in the beta state. Beta occurs when we are highly alert and stimulated. For example, our everyday lives in normal, 100-mph society push us into beta states. Our fear-based society and education system is most certainly strengthened when we live solely in beta.

Alpha, the next state along, is an entirely different world. It can be described as relaxing or meditative. Among its many benefits when compared to a beta state, it:

- improves concentration and clarity of thought,
- increases learning ability and memory,
- improves the immune system,
- stimulates our imagination, our intuition, and higher awareness, and
- allows us peak physical prowess.

In other words, alpha is where it's at. It's the place to be.

Alpha typically occurs when we slow down and spend time in natural settings. It's what happens when we choose Earth-time. We don't even have to do anything—it just happens by itself. Could there be anything easier? All kinds of mental, physical, and spiritual benefits seep into our lives. It is as if we just soak them up by being there. The Earth is a remarkable classroom, educating us all on multiple different levels, spoken and unspoken. She provides the richest learning environment there is.

We require a balance of all four states of being—beta, alpha, theta, and delta—to lead lives of peace, love, joy, and purpose. An excess of any of them will inevitably lead to problems.

Concerning children's learning, it is ironic that the modern system asks children to remember huge amounts of information in beta, which is actually a remarkably inefficient state in which to learn. If schools would slow down the frantic pace and also allow children to spend more time outdoors, they would be more likely to move into an alpha state of being that would be far more effective at helping them produce what the system is asking of them.

Moving on to the last two states, theta can be described as a kind of daydream state, with greater access to creativity. Levels of emotions and spontaneity are increased here. Finally, delta occurs when we are asleep, a time of renewal and regeneration. It is difficult for most people to access these last two states while fully awake but it can be done—deep meditation has been used by many to achieve them. So for the purposes of everyday life and education, we will concentrate on moving away from beta and into alpha. One step at a time for now, and this is the most important step.

Now, I don't go around constantly checking how fast my brain waves are going. Nor do I ask myself if I'm in beta, alpha, theta or delta. But it is beneficial to recognize that our very reality changes as we move from state to state. The dynamic reality we enjoy while in alpha is a completely different world to the sluggishness of beta. These states do not just occur by chance. We are controlling them, either consciously or unconsciously, with the environments we live in and the way in which we go about our everyday lives. So begin to take notice your general state of being. When are you calm, nervous, inspired, or fearful? Notice if different external environments make it easier or more difficult to maintain a positive state of being. It shouldn't take long to figure out some kind of pattern. You could probably work it out right now. Let's say you find being indoors under fluorescent lighting for seven hours at a time to be a difficult place to be creative. If that is the case, we shouldn't expect children to be. If, on the other hand, you find having an adventure in the woods to be very inspiring, it's reasonable to assume the same would be true for children.

Earth-time is the foundation from which children's connection to the natural world can flourish. We obviously should be encouraging them to be in the environments that are most conducive to creativity, higher learning, better health, and clarity of thought. This is the natural world, where children will be able to experience the free and full expression of their being.

TRULY ALIVE TIP 🌿 🌿 🌿 🌿 🌿 🌿

Sit Spot

This tip changes everything. It holds untold riches and is the doorway to a grander, larger reality.

An activity that can truly help children experience love, peace, joy, and purpose is to spend time in their own private "sit spot." This is a place, usually in a natural setting, where children can go and enjoy the show that nature puts on. There are no expectations placed upon the child, and failure is not possible. They don't have to do anything or be anything in their sit spot but simply sit and take in the wonder and beauty all around them.

What makes a good sit spot? It is normally best in a location that has a connection to the Earth. For example, sitting by an apple tree in a garden or in a field of wildflowers, and not in a bedroom; sitting on a rock beside a stream, and not in a classroom. It should be easily accessible. If you have to drive your child for thirty minutes to reach it, or children have to ask for special assistance in getting there, it's probably not going to work in the long-term. Make it somewhere you or the child can easily get to. The individual decides how long to spend at their sit spot, and how often to return. A good goal is once a day for at least ten minutes. More is fine, less is okay. Ultimately, the time is unimportant. The most important thing, especially for children, is that it is an enriching experience. If the child finds anything unappealing about the spot, it's not somewhere they are going to want to return to. A time element is added because it can take several minutes before our minds feel any benefit, before we can slow down and plug into our surroundings.

It is important for children that they do not have outlandish expectations. For example, do they think that when they spend time in nature, a bald eagle will suddenly appear on a branch right next to them, or that a new born deer fawn will wander across their path? Hoping for such Hollywood-type scenes is bound to end in frustration and a sense of failure. If they harbor these expectations, they will miss what is happening in the present moment. There might be a gentle breeze on their cheek, or beautiful birdsong. Whatever is there, you can be assured it will be truly alive, and it will foster the same vibrancy in children.

ॐ ॐ ॐ ॐ ॐ ॐ

Questions to the Earth

Earlier, we looked at encouraging children to ask their own questions and find their own answers. This is particularly important in order to foster independence of thought and action. We are not looking to provide answers, but rather an environment in which children can ask questions and find inspiration for the things they are passionate about. With a new education model, we will naturally seek to guide children to that most remarkable of teachers—the Earth.

So why should children take their questions to the Earth? Because by walking as one with the Earth, children will find love. Children will find that the Earth is unconditional love—giving everything and asking for nothing in return. This will seep into their consciousness, into their very being, and the answers they bring back will be infused with love.

By walking as one with the Earth, children will find peace. They will find the Earth to be peaceful, from her gentlest of streams to her most destructive of storms. If we want to truly commune with life we must embrace all her energies, not just those which serve one tiny portion of life in the form of humans. I remember standing outside recently in hurricane Irene (from a certain point of view, it was not my most sensible act and not something I would recommend) watching the trees almost bend over double, whipped by the ferocious winds. I remember feeling that wind almost blowing me over, the rain coming in sideways and lashing against my face, feeling like hundreds of needles hitting my skin. Yet there in the midst of what we have labeled "destructive" there was great peace. The energy that storm carried was so easily felt it was almost like nature was talking to me. It was communicating to me that it was very much alive, that there was a consciousness flowing through it, like everything in creation, and that to label it "bad" is to demonstrate our lack of awareness that one part of life can ever be superior to any other. When we can look at the destruction that a storm causes and see it as perfect, see it as part of the Oneness, then we will be truly alive. Children will one day fuse with the life-force of all things, calm and destructive, large and small, plant and animal, rock and water, sun and rain, and when they do the answers they bring back will be the embodiment of peace.

By walking as one with the Earth, children will find joy. They will experience joy the likes of which they have never felt before. They will know happiness in all of creation, from the tiniest insect to the soaring of an eagle and from a single grain of sand to the magnificent power of a mountain. Every element of nature will sing to them, and that joy will be felt in the answers they bring back.

And, by being one with the Earth, children will find purpose. They will experience the beautiful dance of life itself. They will find that they have a role, a place, and a glorious purpose beyond their individual selves.

Taking a question to the Earth and seeking an answer is more than just a function of the mind. It is a full-sensory, full-being experience. Everything about the child is engaged: all the senses of the body, mind, and soul. As such, it has real depth and meaning. The child owns the answer, and so it is powerful in every positive sense of the word. The answer becomes their truth.

It's important to remember that the Earth is not providing the answers for children. She is helping them to find the answers that are already within them. This, surely, is being truly alive.

With time and a true connection to the Earth, children can experience all of this and more. Nothing else can bring our young people this depth and meaning that they yearn for so badly. We have seen that our current educational system is unable to break free from the prison it has created for itself. It has failed and it is currently failing our children. Let us return now to the teacher—the Earth—whose answers are more magnificent than most have ever even conceived of, the teacher who is the source of all we need to remember to be truly alive. Let us encourage our children to take their questions to the Earth and then rejoice before even hearing the answers. We know that the Earth will answer, and will answer wisely in her own time. In this way, the limits of our current education system are left behind. In their place come freedom and possibility. We will be able to support children's experiences of life in a way that up to now we have been too fearful to embrace.

As individuals and as a society, we must find the strength and courage to give children the gift of *connection to the natural world*. We can give this gift simply by choosing to do so.

CHAPTER 13

Doing Nothing

Everything starts as somebody's daydream.

~Larry Niven

A Different World

I visit my sit spot often—once a day if I can. It's just a few hundred feet from my home in Colorado, in a ponderosa pine forest, the Rocky Mountains towering all around. I take a slow, fox walk out there, and switch on my senses. As my feet fall gently on the Earth, I feel my whole being shift into a different gear. I notice where the deer left their tracks as they fed, unhurried, enjoying the new green shoots. At the top of a small rise, the ponderosas are calling out to me to press my nose against their bark and smell deeply their intoxicating aroma. To me, it's a perfect butterscotch-and-vanilla scent, and I can never just sniff once and walk away. I return for more until the sound of the mountain stream below beckons me onward. I sit down, against an old tree, looking down at the gently tumbling waters below. I feel the wind against my cheek; it is reassuring and real after too much time spent inside. I let my eyes relax into soft-focus vision, marveling at the difference it creates in my awareness. It feels as if nature has just accepted me as part of her, and all the colors, sounds, and feelings around me are turned to *full*. With my new way of seeing, I become aware of movement everywhere, and I easily pick out a chickadee landing in my peripheral vision. I say hello to my old friend, and he cocks his head to the side as if to nod his greeting too. As always, he doesn't stay still long before he is off on another errand.

In my sit spot, rich in nature, I lose track of time. You could tell me five minutes or one hour had passed and I would believe you. If there is a place where time as we know it does not exist, it must surely be in nature. I feel something about to change, like a small wave coming toward me, and I know this means things are about to happen. I hear a flurry of birdcalls from the south, and those birds that usually feed on the ground hop into the trees. The wave is about to come crashing down around me, and then it breaks. A red fox, her fur glistening in the sunlight, trots past, stops for a second when she catches my scent, then is on her way back to her den after a hunting expedition. My mind is at peace, and I am calm—happy for no particular reason I can think of. There is a feeling, an unspoken understanding, that something more than myself is all around me, all-embracing and loving. I know I am connected, and I understand my purpose and place in the great rhythm of life.

Most of all, I am inspired: ideas come easily. From where they come I don't know, and it doesn't really matter. Maybe they come from within because I can listen properly, or maybe they come from outside. Either way, they are with me, and I am grateful. Seeds are nourished and grow well. I founded an organization from my sit spot, wrote this book, and, most importantly, rediscovered my love for life.

All that just from sitting still. To those who haven't tried it for more than a few days, I suppose it could seem lazy, but to me it is common sense, the most productive time of my day, and the perfect way to experience who I really am.

Time to Reflect

As part of the *free* and *full* culture of experience, it is vital that children be given time to reflect. Let's return to that two-part question, the doorway to a life of real purpose:

- What happened here?
- What does this mean to me?

As children ask this, they will naturally find answers that will be experienced on many different levels. Those levels or layers within each answer are likely to reveal themselves at different speeds. Some layers may become apparent immediately, while others might not reveal themselves for months or even years.

This is important to acknowledge because children need time to rearrange their minds. In truth, they will actually need time to rearrange far more than just their thinking about new answers. They will feel a natural pressure from within to rearrange their very being—all aspects of themselves—body, mind, and soul. With each new experience they become someone new. Does this support who I was before? Where does this fit in with who I believe I am? Does this change my beliefs about life? While children may not consciously ask the questions in these exact words, on some level they are being deeply considered. Some changes could be small; others could be seismic. They may need to lay entire foundations of new belief systems. This could take weeks, months, or years.

Imagine planting a new garden. You don't just hurriedly throw all the plants in one big pile, frantically adding to the heap as often as you can. No, taking your time is best. First, you plant the flowers and trees you think will grow well. Then you sit back, watch, and observe. The seasons come and go. Maybe a tree grows more quickly and to a larger size than you had expected. Because of this, flowers may need to be moved to get a little more sunlight. After a few months you decide to move a whole shrub, wanting something different there. After a few years of growing the garden, you learn about soil quality, so you add some rich compost. Plant, grow, trim, nurture. It's always an ongoing experience; it's never finished. New information comes in. You need time to think, to organize yourself, and decide who you are in relation to this new information and new experiences. It cannot and does not happen instantly.

Time to daydream, to stare at clouds, or sit under a tree is not wasted time. It is very much needed for a child to be able to make the most of each new experience. Thich Nhat Hanh says in *Answers from the Heart* (Parralax Press, 2009) that "Doing nothing brings about quality of being, which is very important." Time for doing nothing needs to become a part of the new culture. Time away from the teacher and time away from other societal stimuli is a good thing. This reflective time is crucial for a child to be balanced and healthy. From this place of balance flow love, peace, joy, and purpose.

Reflective time is also exceptionally important because it is when we so often find inspiration. The world always needs new ideas and creative thinkers. Time spent allowing the mind to wander freely is a wonderful catalyst for ideas to come seemingly from nowhere. But of course the ideas were always there—they just never had the time or opportunity to develop and float to the surface amid all the "proper" learning that was taking place.

Not only does the current system see no need for reflective time for children, there is no place for it within the system. This is not something you can schedule. "Class 2B will take their reflective time from 2:00 p.m. to 2:30 p.m. on Thursday afternoons." As you read the previous sentence, it immediately sounds ridiculous. This is not advocating the absence of all routines. We all need some routines in our lives. But, what we need even more than routines is balance. Children, especially teenagers, should be able to decide for themselves when they need reflective time. Some days we just feel like we need time to settle our minds and only the individual knows exactly when this is.

Children do not have to be forever doing something. Constant activity does not lead to wisdom, or to the soul. Both of these are experienced through a balanced life and time simply being.

Friend or Foe?

We must ask ourselves if, as individuals and as a society, we are helping our children's minds to be their best friend or their worst enemy. Can you hear that little voice in your head? It's the one that provides the running commentary to our lives. If you can't hear it right now, just stop reading for a few moments—and do nothing. It'll pop up without fail, asking, demanding that you fill the space with something, anything. Our minds need constant distraction because they are so out of control. And naturally, our children grow up needing and seeking the same distractions as we do.

Some people have called that little voice the ego, the small self, and one that I personally love—"duct-tape man." Jon Young, a proponent of Coyote Teaching, has coined that name for the voice because it can drive us so insane that all we want to do is cover it with duct tape to shut it up. It can indeed be our greatest friend, but more often than not, given the way we live, it is our biggest foe. As soon as we are not doing something, in it jumps. It has us frantically searching for something to *do* in order that we stay in its world. Organize the sock drawer, check the sports scores, watch television, call a friend, even keep reading these words. Do, do, do—that little voice demands that you *do* something to fill the void in your life.

Try doing nothing: just be still for a few moments. It can genuinely be excruciatingly painful. It can have you feeling like you are going out of your mind. Unfortunately, it is painful because we are addicted to the small mind, and ignoring it brings on withdrawal effects. We have fed our addiction to such a degree, neglecting all other states of mind, that it has a certain type of control over us. Our entire society is organized around being distracted from who we really are.

How can our children ever live in a peaceful world if they are constantly in a battle with their own minds? How can our children ever lead lives of deep purpose if the only thing they seek is to be distracted from who they really are? As always, our outer world is a direct representation of our inner world. If we don't like what we see in the outside world we must go within to find out why we created it.

For many of the children I come into contact with, if we ask them to simply be still for just a few seconds and enjoy the show that nature puts on, many are unable to do so. You can literally feel and see their pain as soon as they don't have a distraction to keep their minds at bay. It does not make for pleasant viewing.

Given time and support, children can learn to let go of much of that need for distraction. One homeschool group I worked with found it amazingly painful to be still in their sit spot for even a few minutes. We started off by making the time just being still into a game, and this got most of them over that first hurdle of lacking physical distractions for the mind to feast on. It took us six months of working gently but persistently with those children to turn the sit spot activity from one that elicited groans into the highlight of the day for many. The children named it "Chill-Out Time." Every single one of us wants to find peace of mind, but the paths we create in society lead us far away from it.

If we had a chance to ensure that our children did not suffer from painful addiction to that little voice of the ego, wouldn't we want to grasp that opportunity with both hands and do our utmost to make it happen? The solution is as simple as doing nothing, and just being who and what we really are.

As individuals and as a society, we must find the strength and courage to give children the gift of *time and space simply to be.* We can give this gift by choosing to do so.

CHAPTER 14

Adventures and How to Support Them

If you want to build a ship, don't drum up people to collect
wood and don't assign them tasks and work, but rather teach
them to long for the endless immensity of the sea.

~Antoine de Saint-Exupéry

Ellie and the Blindfold Drum Stalk

As the sun is going down and darkness is just beginning to creep over the landscape, one of my very favorite activities to share with a group of people, particularly children, is something called a "blindfold drum stalk." It's very simple. The participants are led out into the woods. The last few hundred feet of this journey they are blindfolded,

191

and they will remain so for about twenty to thirty minutes. Multiple adults are posted along all parts of their route so, although the participants cannot see, they are as safe as anyone can be walking slowly in the woods. All is quiet. They are waiting for the sound of a drum to start beating, somewhere distant in the woods. As soon as they hear it, they start to walk slowly—because of their blindfolds—toward the sound of the drum, "stalking" its sound. The drum beats approximately once every seven or eight seconds, so mostly it is very quiet. The participants are walking through the woods, seemingly isolated, as if in the dark of night, and the only thing they have to guide them is a distant drum. They could walk into trees, hit bushes or cobwebs, stumble over rocks, or worse still, be left out in the woods by themselves. I've done the blindfold drum stalk myself, and can say with all honesty that it can be very scary indeed. The difference between this fear and the fear that stems from our misunderstandings about life is that I was given, and I always give others, the tools they need to move beyond their fears. This way the exercise does not become paralyzing, but something that can be used to great effect for personal growth.

The following story is about a girl who came to one of the programs I was running. Ellie was just twelve when she had a remarkable experience with the drum stalk.

Ellie came to the program with her mother and had been with us in the woods for four days. In that brief time, she had learned many new skills and nature awareness techniques that had taken her outside her comfort zone, but tonight was going to be the ultimate test for her.

Everyone gathered round the campfire just as the sun was beginning to touch the horizon. About twenty people would be blindfolded, and almost as many "protectors" would make sure everyone was safe in their unique experience in the woods. I explained the activity to everyone, deliberately making it sound more risky than it was. The blindfold drum stalk is based loosely on an activity the Apaches used to help their young ones become scouts—the eyes and ears of the tribe—the ultimate service. The young Apaches undoubtedly had a far more arduous task than we were going to ask of our campers, but by telling them the story I wanted them to make comparisons and believe that this was going to be the test to end all tests. After all, just walking through the woods at night is scary enough for most people, but here we were telling them they would be blindfolded as well.

In reality, the exercise placed people in no danger whatsoever. The worst that could happen was they might move a little too quickly and trip or bump into a branch or something similar. However, if it wasn't a challenge, and if they weren't outside their comfort zone, they wouldn't be able to grow. The people who were about to put on blindfolds built this up in their minds to be a seriously risky adventure, but I had given them the tools they needed (including fox walking, and the understanding they needed to surrender to what the forest was telling them) in order to succeed and to move beyond their fears. I knew from experience that those tools would be used to great effect.

Ellie was right on the edge. More than anyone else in the group, she had built up the idea of this activity in her mind and then became doubtful she could achieve it, even with the tools she had been given. She approached me, saying she didn't want to do it. When I asked her why, she could not give an explanation. Obviously she was scared, so I took the time to explain to her how it had been for me when I did it. I told her I had also been scared, but I remembered what I had been told—to fox walk and to surrender to the woods—and that after a few steps, I forgot to be scared, and it had turned into an amazing, life-changing experience. I could tell she really wanted to do it, and so we agreed that she would follow everyone else out, and then make up her mind at the last minute. This seemed to sit well with her, and so she joined the end of the line of intrepid adventurers on their walk out into the woods. I had seen a number of children in a similar situation to Ellie, most of whom had managed to overcome their fears, but I was not so sure with Ellie. I thought she might let hers get the better of her.

I left her to go to the spot where I began beating the drum. After about ten minutes I began to see the first few people walking slowly, sensing and feeling their way to the drum's beat. I was looking for Ellie, hoping she wouldn't be bringing up the rear un-blindfolded with a member of staff. Almost everyone had made it safely to the drum, as they always do. Quietly, I asked one of the members of the staff to tell me how many more people were still coming in to the drum. She returned a few moments later to tell me there were four, one of whom was Ellie. Fantastic!

Ellie was not at the back of the bunch because she was scared— exactly the opposite: as she had fox walked and become aware of the present moment she had experienced a great sense of calm and deep peace. As she finished and removed her blindfold, her face exploded with pride and immense satisfaction. She came up to me, smiling from ear to ear. I could almost feel her energy buzzing as she said simply, "I did it." I was as happy for her as she was for herself.

Ellie came back the next year. She told me how the adventure of the blindfold drum stalk had changed her as a person. She explained to me that now, when she's afraid, she fox walks and tells herself it will be okay. She still has fear but she knows she can conquer it because she remembers how much fun the blindfold test was. Ellie's adventure outside her comfort zone was both life enhancing and quite typical. All the children I have seen who also conquered their fear grew immensely from the experience.

Learning From the Coyote

Let's bring in the remarkable coyote. In many Native American cultures the coyote is seen as a trickster. There are endless stories with the coyote manipulating a situation that sees him (it is almost always referred to as a male) getting the better of adversaries who are less wily than he. Intriguingly, the coyote is also often considered to be the keeper of knowledge who plays a sort of grandfather role, guiding humans toward their own growth. We, as mentors to children, can learn a lot from the ways of the coyote.

Whenever I have encountered a coyote it has always been in a similar place in relation to me. Usually they don't lie still like rabbits do, waiting for me to almost step on them before bolting out into the forest. Typically I am straining from a distance to get a better view, and suddenly they are gone. If I were out walking with a friend, I'd probably turn to them and say, "Wow! Was that a coyote? I'm sure I just glimpsed it as it moved through the trees." The coyote is on the periphery, on the edge of things, and highly elusive. We catch fleeting glimpses that tantalize us because they are just out of reach.

Our experiences with the coyote form a perfect model for how we can encourage and support children to grow without forcing them. We can do this by imagining positioning ourselves in a child's educa-tion in a similar manner to how the coyote interacts with us; on the edge of awareness. Let's use an example to illustrate this reposition-ing. Imagine a boy is learning the piano. A facilitator is working with the boy to help him experience playing the piano the best he possibly can. If the facilitator simply listens to the boy play, and then points out every mistake, the facilitator is occupying the same space as the child, rather than being on the edge of his awareness. There are cer-tainly times when this is necessary, but if this is the only way the boy is taught, he is unlikely to progress much beyond the physical act of pushing the keys to make a sound. Like everything else in life, we re-quire a balance. The way we support children is no different. Imagine now if the facilitator moves to the edge of the boy's awareness. Maybe one day the teacher plays a piece that is slightly too difficult for the boy right now but, while playing, works into the piece the things the boy needs to improve. So maybe the facilitator exaggerates the distinction between loud and quiet, fast and slow, making them more easily recognized by the boy. If the facilitator plays with passion, the young apprentice will surely want to emulate his teacher's skill, and either consciously or unconsciously will begin to adopt these advanced techniques in his own playing. The facilitator is supporting from the edge of the child's awareness.

Imagine if one day they sit outside, away from the piano, and the facilitator talks to the boy about feeling music all around him. Can he feel the melodies in his emotions? Can he feel a rhythm in the way people move in the city? Can he feel his own path, guiding him to the notes he must play? It is likely that the boy did not realize some of these things were even possible, but now he has been given a glimpse of something that was previously outside his realm of awareness. This plants seeds that continue to germinate and grow for months and years. The facilitator is supporting the child from the edge, helping him to see a more distant horizon, and then giving him the tools to make it a reality.

Keith Richards, a guitarist with the Rolling Stones, once taught me (not personally, unfortunately) from the very edge of my awareness. He was asked what he thought about while he was playing music on stage. "Think? I don't think. I feel. If you think, you're screwed!" I have not stopped learning from that one simple statement to this day. He was not instructing anybody, nor was he occupying the same space as the listener, but he gave those who heard him speak something to aspire to in the short-term, and something to really make you think deep and hard about life itself in the long-term.

The way of the coyote in a teaching environment is to appear as one thing on the surface, but for multiple layers to reveal themselves slowly to the student over time. A student who is taught using the coyote method can never say they have ever completely finished learning from a lesson; there is always another layer to discover. Tom Brown Jr. is one of the most remarkable teachers I have ever met. When I first learned from him, I understood what he was saying on one level, which helped me to learn what was at hand. But the longer I spent around him, and the longer those seeds had to germinate, the greater my realization that he had also taught me from way beyond the edge of my awareness. His knowledge and wisdom showed me there was more that I didn't yet fully understand, but that, with the tools he had given me, both physical and non-physical, I could expand my own awareness. I have the rest of my life to push my edge to reach all the nuances and meanings he taught me, which at the time I was hardly aware of.

So the most effective teachers are in three places at once. They are *here*. This means being right beside the student, helping a child from moment to moment to achieve the next small goal, learn the next fact, and correct mistakes. (This is the only one of the three locations of a great teacher that we truly follow in mainstream education).

An inspiring teacher is also *there*. As we have just seen, a great facilitator is also found on the edge of a child's awareness, planting the seeds that create depth for years to come.

Lastly, if children are given the tools with which to be independent in their learning, there is never a time that they are alone on their paths. The teacher's positive influence is always with them, *everywhere*.

Coyote Teaching promotes independence in the learner because it stimulates constant questions. When everything is plain and simple, as most learning is in our current system, we ask a simple question, get a simple answer, and that's that. There is very little depth to the whole experience. With Coyote Teaching, because many of the questions, answers and observations made by the teacher are right on the edge of the student's awareness, children begin to think critically for themselves. They question what they have been told, they test it to see if it's really true, and in doing so, they learn independently.

Teaching in the coyote method allows children to walk their own individual paths. In our earlier example of the facilitator asking the child if he could feel the melodies in his own emotions, the student was not being told what to do. On the contrary, he was being encouraged to follow his own vision, his own ideas, thoughts and feelings.

Most importantly, a student of a Coyote Teacher never stops learning—is never "done". The adventure is a lifelong journey. The edge of the learner's awareness is constantly being challenged and extended, even without the physical presence of the teacher.

Given that our goal is to guide children to the freest and fullest experience of life we possibly can, facilitators who embrace Coyote Teaching would be continually trying to find out where the edge of the child's awareness is. When they understand this, they know far better how they may be able to support the child to expand it. Coyote Teachers look for ways they can allow children a glimpse of what is beyond their current edge, so that a desire and a passion will be created in them to become more, to reach out for a new experience beyond that current boundary of awareness. In this way, Coyote Teachers create opportunities for children's souls to experience life to the full.

If we, as teachers, work on an agenda, trying to push a skill or a subject on a child, that child is likely—especially in the long term—to turn away from it. The coyote teaches us to work with children's passions, nudging them in the direction of the passion, not forcing our agendas upon them. Our role as facilitators is to place experiences in front of children, then watch and observe what they do with them. Do they turn away, or do they ask for more? It is important that we keep placing new and different experiences in front of children. After all, if you don't know something exists, how can you be passionate about it? If you never knew you could paint with watercolors, how could you be passionate about it? If no one ever shared with you the joy of reading, why would you pick up a book?

We can take three easy steps to support children in this truly alive culture:

1. Continually expose children to new and different experiences.
2. Watch and observe what they do with these experiences. What are their choices? Do they choose more of the same, or do they choose something different?
3. Whatever they choose, the role of the facilitator is to find ways to encourage children to push the edges of their own awareness without the children realizing they are being encouraged.

Our current model also seeks to have children grow and become more. However, it is a system that pushes and prods children to do so. Knowledge is pushed down their throats so hard and fast they scarcely have time to catch their breaths and ask their own questions. If a child shows signs of rebellion and wanting to jump ship, certain predictable lines are brought out. These are almost always fear based. "You will be a failure" or "You won't get a good job" are two that are regularly used by educational establishments. We should be clear that if we want our children to reach a destination of love, peace, joy, and purpose, the path along the way also has to embody these qualities. The coyote method is gentle yet powerful, subtle yet strong. It teaches without forcing, guides without overwhelming, and inspires the body, mind and soul each day to understand and experience what it is to be truly alive.

From Straight Lines to Spheres

When I have run programs for adults to introduce them to teaching using the way of the coyote, to teach from the three different areas of discovery (*here*, *there* and *everywhere*), the participants almost always begin to find that their relationships with children take on new meanings. They can be moved to a different reality. A good analogy is that we can move teaching from a world of straight lines to a world of spheres. We currently have a paradigm of straight-line teaching. The children are at point A, and we need to move them to point B. They should complete this journey as quickly as possible, with every child being moved in exactly the same manner, year after year. Education is effectively treading the same path in a straight line, year after year. It's no wonder we have created ruts we can't see out of. Life for children has become the equivalent of the caged tiger in the zoo, pacing along the same stretch of ground, creating ever deeper ruts along its path. That beautiful animal, just like the minds of children, is kept confined to a small box, never knowing or able to realize its true potential.

The straight line also enables hierarchies to exist. These create all sorts of problems that stem from illusions of superiority. A college-educated person is considered superior to a high-school graduate, and any kind of human—educated or not—is considered superior to any other part of nature. This is based on the value we place upon "cleverness" and learning facts. We consider ourselves superior because we believe ourselves to be cleverer. Yet it is not the "stupid" animals of nature that have brought our society to the brink of self-destruction. And it will not necessarily be our college-educated humans who meet the challenges we face. It will be the people who are brave enough to leave the straight-line world behind.

Straight lines are human inventions. Try to find one in nature; to my knowledge they don't exist. Nature teaches us that everything moves in circles and cycles, and it is a wise person who learns and shares this. The Coyote Teacher supports children in the language of the natural world—circles and spheres. And where do you start in a sphere, and where do you go? Anywhere you please! No journeys are better than or superior to other ones. The Coyote Teacher guides children to exploring their own spheres of awareness and encourages them to grow in any way they choose. Where are they going? That's for them to decide along the way.

The way of the coyote is gentle yet powerful, simple yet complex. It holds the key for us to support children in a far more conscious and positive way. It challenges us as adults, constantly encouraging us to become more aware of the beautiful souls we are interacting with.

Adventures

Adventures are the body's way of feeling exhilarated as adrenaline and endorphins are released. They are the mind's way of feeling inspired. They are the soul's way of jumping for joy. Most of all, adventures are the way in which we celebrate being alive! And this is what humans seek to do more than any other thing—to experience life to its fullest. We all need adventures—children and adults alike.

Adventures come in all shapes and sizes. An adventure might be chasing a butterfly around the garden, or scaling Mount Everest. It might be working out the final move in a game of chess, or finding a cure for AIDS. It might be experiencing happiness for a loved one, or experiencing oneness with all that is.

What all adventures have in common is that they allow us to experience something new for ourselves. As a result of the experience, we feel alive because our body, mind and soul have discovered a greater reality. We grow so much and on so many levels through the adventures that we have. They can be even more powerful when we throw in another element—being outside our comfort zone. This takes the form of all manner of experiences, each highly personal to the individual. For some, a new social situation could push them to the edge of their comfort zone. For others, it could be sleeping outside for the first time. One thing we all have in common is that each of us has our own comfort zone.

In going outside our comfort zone, an element of fear may be involved as well. Quitting a job could lead an individual to experience fear, as could parachuting from an airplane for the first time. Being outside our comfort zones and being fearful are really the same thing. I'm using fear to denote extreme cases of being outside a particular comfort zone. But please don't think that every adventure has to be terrifying. The adventures in which children are outside their comfort zones or on the edge of fear and then succeed are vitally important because they can see instantly that they have become a new person. They experience vividly that they are indeed alive. But not only that. They also have the experience of actually becoming more, of physically moving out of their old selves and into the new. They have the perception of becoming more alive; they are expanding their awareness. They were always more than they thought they were; they just weren't aware of it. There is an understanding on their part that if they can do it once, they can do it again and again and again. It satisfies the soul like nothing else can.

If this kind of experience is repeated from an early age, children learn that fear can be transformed from something that paralyzes into something that inspires. It inspires them to feel fear and then to go beyond, leaving it behind. It is worth repeating that we must equip children with the tools to move beyond their fears, especially if we are the ones instigating a move to the edge of their comfort zone. Otherwise the outcome is left too much to chance. With luck the child might find a way past their fears. But equally likely, without first being given the tools to do this, they might find that the fear not only stays with them but also grows into something quite paralyzing. We want to ensure children actually feel the edge, but can then take control of the situation and move beyond it.

Children hear the call of their souls asking them to come and play, and they answer without hesitation. Observe very young children. They are the epitome of being alive. Everything is an adventure to them.

But as they grow older, it becomes obvious that children learn, from somewhere, to begin to silence that voice to a barely audible whisper. What is happening? Why are adventures put aside as children grow into adults? Fear is happening, plain and simple. We have allowed and are continuing to allow fear to dominate our lives, and we pass this straight on to our children. As adults we still hear the call of our souls, but fear overrides it, having not been controlled or put in its place. Instead, our fears grow strong from constantly being fed, so we move ever closer to being paralyzed, and further away from being inspired.

Young people, especially teenagers, are showing by their actions that they are seeking adventure. Across society, they play out a whole range of activities designed to help them experience something new. Some go exploring to far-off countries. Others take part in extreme sports such as bungee jumping, skydiving, and whitewater rafting. Still other teens get their adventures on the wrong side of the law. This can take many forms, including driving fast, taking drugs, or committing crimes.

For all of these adventures, children have numerous reasons for making the choices they do. But all these activities are undoubtedly undertaken because they allow children to experience more—to become more alive. It can be argued that by denying children opportunities for real adventure, we have as a society pushed them toward the more dangerous and destructive end of the examples given. It doesn't matter how much we try to control young people's behavior, the need for adventure is never going to leave them completely, because their souls are never going to leave them. That need can come out in a healthy, creative manner. Or it can form the energy behind extremely destructive actions.

As adults, we have a responsibility to help our children respond to the call of adventure. It is not going to go away. We can encourage them and provide a relatively safe environment in which they can have positive, full, and free experiences.

204 · Adventures and how to Support Them

How can we improve the chances of this happening? By under-standing that adventures are not just for children! We too must play and be alive. As adults we can also embrace the experience of becoming more. But that cannot happen unless we refuse to allow fear to paralyze us. Adventures must be consciously chosen, and the spirit of adventure must be passed on to our children. We must allow children to have their own adventures, find their edge, and then go beyond. We need to stop wrapping them in cotton wool every single minute of the day. Instead, let them get muddy, dirty, and wet. Let them be hot and cold, tired and awake. Let them be happy, sad, angry, and joyous. In this way, they will leave fear behind and become all the things they can dream of. I am not for one moment suggesting we place children in dangerous situations where they could harm themselves or others. But we must allow them to be fully alive. Otherwise, why are they here?

As individuals and as a society, we must find the strength and courage to give children the gift of *seeking and embracing adventure*. We can give this gift by choosing to do so.

It is important to recognize that adventures need to be balanced with the reflective, "doing nothing" time we discussed in Chapter 12. Moving outside our comfort zone should form a healthy ebb and flow with this quieter, more reflective time. Neither having constant adventures nor the opposite—doing nothing all the time—will be beneficial for the child in the long run. There has to be time to reflect on the adventures in order for them to have the best effect on the in-dividual. That is why a balance of adventures and reflective time form a perfect partnership.

CHAPTER 15

Seven Generations

A society grows great when old men plant trees whose
shade they know they shall never sit in.
~Greek proverb

The Gifts

If we can find the strength and courage to give our children the
following gifts, their lives will be transformed into glorious expres-
sions of who they truly are. They will not only experience, but they
will *become* love, peace, joy, and purpose. Can we allow them a full
life experience? Can we set them free to be truly alive? We can begin
by giving these gifts:

- Teach that we are all one.
- Provide education that exists for the free and full expression
  of the individual.
- Honor every child's uniqueness.

- Allow children to measure their own success.
- Help children understand that everyone has a unique gift to give.
- Model living in the present.
- Facilitate independence.
- Assist children in discovering the beauty of questions.
- Encourage children to find and live their own truths.
- Support children to experience their natural connection with the Earth.
- Allow children time and space simply to be.
- Encourage children to seek and embrace adventure.

All of these gifts can be summarized in just two concepts: *freedom and love*. And when you set someone free, you are giving them unconditional love. Thus, we really come down to one simple, beautiful gift: *love*.

Can we give the gift of love? Can we give this gift in every moment, in every thought, in every word we speak, and in all of our actions? Can we give the gift of love so that we can give the gift of being truly alive?

Looking Our Fears in the Face

A few key traits would serve us well, regardless of the manner in which we wish to support children in their lives. The first is to listen to and observe what children are telling us. We don't have to ask them direct questions, but simply observe what they are telling us with their actions. From there we have two choices: to impose our will upon them, as we currently do, or to give them space to walk their own paths.

If we allow children to chart their own paths in life, what do we fear they are going to do that is so "wrong"? If we don't prescribe a path for them, what are children going to do that will make the lives of adults unbearable?

The need to impose our will and our agenda on children stems from allowing fear to get the better of us. This fear shrinks our beliefs and encourages us to think small thoughts. They are small because our ideas about ourselves are literally less. When fear overtakes us, we forget that we are connected to all things. We do not live as though we are all one. This inevitably creates a very different environment for children than if we look at fear and say, "No, thank you. Today I am more than fear. Today I am life itself."

So a big step, possibly the largest in creating a life experience for children that sees them reconnected with life, is to look at our own fears. If we adults cannot begin to leave our fears behind, we are condemning children to the same fate. We must do anything it takes to break this cycle. Read books, meditate, talk to one another, listen to one another, fox walk, visit sit spots, give thanks, play games.

Above all, to create a new world we must become conscious of who we really are—an eternal, divine being, who flows with and through the whole of life, connected to every last piece of energy in the universe. We are not our packaging—our body, our thoughts, our jobs, our beliefs, or even our success, but we are pure *being*. Now and forever. We may move with the cycles of life, we may live consciously or unconsciously, but we can rest assured that we will always simply *be*. If we act from a place of pure *being* there is nothing that can prevent us creating love, peace, joy, and purpose for our children in every sacred moment of their lives.

It should be clear that in a world without separation we are never alone. Among our fellow humans there are hundreds and thousands of people who can help us look at fear and understand that it does not have to paralyze us. Fear is a form of suffering, and we have already seen that, should we choose to relate to it differently, it can be a tool and a signpost to point us toward great healing and growth.

When you find support, make sure that it contains one simple message: we are all one, everything is interconnected, there is no separation. These all point to the same truth. Yes, it is different from what most of society is telling us. Does that mean it is not the truth? Only you can decide that.

Fear will always be with us. It is what we do in response to fear that is important. When we feel it, we can decide just for a short time not to pass it on to children, and then see what happens. We can experiment by finding out how their experience of life changes in the absence of fear. We can let them *be* who they are. If we are patient and allow children time and space to be creative, if we are supportive and encourage them to follow the voice of their soul, if we are loving and allow them to be free, children will experience their own truth: that life is a playground and we are free to enjoy every single minute of it. They will be safe, and they will be secure. There is nothing they will have to fight each other for, and nothing they will have to fear. This is freedom. This is truly living.

The Difficult Road Becomes Easy

It should be clear that the ideas put forward in this book are not only to be considered on a physical and mental level. Love, peace, joy, and purpose remain out of reach because right now our spiritual lives are out of reach. Or, more accurately, because we have not reached inside ourselves to find them. Yet they are but a simple choice away. If we are to create the lives that so many of us dream of, we must also include the spiritual—our soul—in any choices we make. We must allow it to be the central part of our belief system. Without the balance of body, mind, and soul, these dreams will never be reality. Yes, some, if not all, of these choices may be scary for us right now. Some may challenge us, and fear could make us want to take what might seem like the easier road.

We must resist making choices that are purely short-term fixes and choices that do not include the soul. Really, these are the same thing, and they both are the epitome of the easier road. We must avoid this at all costs; otherwise, it may cost our children their home and friendship with the Earth. It will certainly cost them their chance to be truly alive. Soon we will see that it is not in fact the easier road. It is very difficult indeed to look at the truth and then ignore it by doing completely the opposite of what life is telling us. We currently look at life and see and feel that we have a soul, and we know deep down that all our souls are connected together, and then we act as if the opposite were true. Soon, this denial becomes the difficult road, the impossible road, because personal experience will always prove more powerful than the words of others.

Martin Luther King Jr. had a dream that white children and black children would play together hand in hand. At the time, there were many who shared his dream. But there were also many who thought that this type of freedom would lead to the destruction of our world. Of course, to the extent that Dr. King's dream came to fruition, it has hugely enriched our world. We see and feel in our hearts that we should choose more freedom in our lives, not less.

Now we have a dream that children can walk hand in hand with life. A dream that love is their friend, that peace joins them together, that they play with joy, and that they are filled with a purpose that knows no limits. We can create this dream. We can create this reality. There should not be a shadow of doubt in our minds that it will happen. The questions are when and how it will happen.

You already know what you have to offer. Talk to other people, form groups of like-minded parents, facilitators, and communities. Offer to share your passions with a group of children once a year or five days a week, or anywhere in between. Look deeply at all aspects of children's lives and ask questions. Question everything including the education system, the beliefs we pass on to children, and especially the ideas presented in this book. This will lead you to your own truths, and from there the possibilities are endless. We create masterpieces from our own truths!

Above all, create consciously with the understanding that we are all one. There is no reason to attack anyone or make someone else fearful. There is no reason to put anyone else down. Instead, choose now to be that path of love, peace, joy, and purpose. As you become that path, others will surely follow. Our dreams will no longer have to be only dreams—they will be our children's lives.

You may be thinking, this is all very well, but how is change on the level this book is proposing actually going to happen? The governments of the world will never change to the degree we want them to, or embrace many of the book's most basic premises, and so we are stuck making minor, almost irrelevant changes to our current system.

This is a simple book. Life is simple. It is we humans who make it complicated. Some of us turn to the gods of science and hope and pray that clever people in white coats can invent something to solve all our problems. Others turn to various religious gods and hope and pray that the divine will be save us. Still others turn to the gods of politics, voting for anyone who promises "change" or "hope". We know in our hearts that things need to change, but we don't know how to do so for ourselves, so we become reliant on others to create change for us. Then when it doesn't happen we become disillusioned with those who promised so much but delivered so little. Out with those who failed us, and in with the next ones.

There is only one place in the entire universe that can create the change we hope for and need: within ourselves. The world we see around us will only change when our most basic beliefs about life change. These changes must take place first on a *being* level, not a *doing* level. Being gives birth to doing. Doing stems from what we are being. When we are being certain things, it is impossible to do certain actions. For example, when we are being truly joyful it is impossible to worry ourselves to death about the future. When we are being truly peaceful it is impossible to harm another sentient being. As we change what we are being, our old ways of doing will simply fall away. They will become completely unsustainable, as our outer world always becomes the image and creation of our inner world. This is as inevitable as the sun rising and setting, and the ocean tides coming and going. We can count on it (at least for a few million more years in the case of the sun and tides).

To create a new way of being, we must allow our beliefs to become fluid. The ability to look at the same thing, but perceive it differently, provides the opportunity for a new belief, a new way of being, to grow and develop. That is what fox walking, soft-focus vision, gratitude, sit spots, using your imagination, and all the other tips, techniques and ideas presented in this book support us in doing. The world still looks, smells and feels the same whether you believe we are separate from each other, or all connected in a sea of energy. But our perception, our being, is in a different universe. What you do when you perceive and *be* in a world of separation is light years away from what you do when you perceive and *be* in a world of connection.

No book, no teacher, and no idea, no matter how remarkable, can create change in our being. They can all lead us to a different path, or make us aware of a new door, but it is we who have to move, we who have to experience something different in order to *be* different. We have to be open and willing to allow our old self to fall away and a new one to emerge.

As we change who we are being it is an absolute certainty that what we do will not remain the same. We will not educate our children in the same way. We will not tell them the same stories, or pass on the same beliefs. We will not create the same society. That is why there is always hope for humankind. Even in our darkest hour, we always have the choice to change who and what we are being. Our children will still grow up on the same Earth, but they will live in a different universe. We don't need money, power, fame, qualifications, government initiatives, or anyone else to do anything for us. If we change who we are being, we will change the world.

Seven Generations

When making choices, the people of the great Iroquois Nation hold a vision in their minds, and consider the implications of their actions upon the next seven generations to come. Not for three or five years, as some of us manage to plan, but for the next *seven generations*. The Iroquois consider what effect their thoughts, words, and deeds will have, not only on their own lives and those of their children, but for their many descendants that they will never meet.

If we continue in the same direction we are going, what kind of lives are we creating for our children, our grandchildren, and the generations to follow? When you consider this deeply, when you really take the time and energy to observe objectively and ask questions without deciding the answers in advance, how do you feel? Your mind will tell you anything to keep you happy, but what do your heart and your soul tell you?

Imagine that your unborn grandchildren are standing before you. Can you look them in the eye and tell them you did everything you could to help them be truly alive, to be full of love, peace, joy, and purpose? If you cannot do this—and not many can—it is time for you to create change.

Change begins with only one person: you. It can only ever begin in one time, and that time is now. Very soon, those next seven generations will be here, on Earth, in the society we have built. What will we have created for them? What legacy will we have left?

Children are crying out for us to understand who they really are. We are all crying out for love, peace, joy, and purpose to be abundant in our lives. Life is crying out for us to return to the simplest and most powerful truth there is: that we are all one. If we still do not have the willpower as adults to create a better life for ourselves, maybe, just maybe, we will find the strength to do so for the generations to come.

Let us conclude by getting right to the heart of the matter. What experiences will you create for a child, right now, in each moment?

What will you say?

Where will you go?

What will you do?

How will you act?

What will you want from them?

and

How will you support them to be truly alive?

Further Reading and Resources

This resource and reading list is limited only to those books, programs and organizations that I have personally found to be highly effective and inspirational and may also provide you with tools to consciously create change. The subject areas are diverse, hopefully allowing you to continue you and your children's growth in a direction you are passionate about.

A Course In Miracles, Foundation For Inner Peace (1976)

The Complete Conversations With God by Neale Donald Walsch
  Putnam Adult (2005)

Coyote's Guide To Connecting With Nature by Jon Young, Evan McGowan
  & Ellen Haas, Owlink Media (2010)

Feel The Fear... and Do It Anyway by Susan Jeffers, Ballantine Books
  (2006–20th Anniversary Edition)

Hands Of Light: A Guide To Healing Through The Human Energy Field by Barbara Ann Brennan, Bantam (1988)

The Hidden Messages In Water by Masaru Emoto, Atria (2005)

Illusions: The Adventures of a Reluctant Messiah by Richard Bach, Random House Group Ltd (1977)

John Muir In His Own Words Compiled & Edited by Peter Browning, Great West Books (1988)

Jonathon Livingston Seagull by Richard Bach, Scribner (2006)

Last Child In The Woods by Richard Louv, Algonquin Books (Updated and Expanded edition 2008)

The Power Of Now: A Guide To Spiritual Enlightenment by Eckhart Tolle New World Library (2004)

Remember, Be Here Now by Ram Dass, Hanuman Foundation (1971)

Savor: Mindful Eating, Mindful Life Thich Nhat Hahn & Lilian Cheung HarperOne (2011)

Tao Te Ching – Lao Tzu translated by Stephen Addiss & Stanley Lombardo, Hackett Publishing Company Inc (1993)

Teenage Liberation Handbook: How to Quit School and Get a Real Life and Education by Grace Llewellyn, Lowry House Publishing (1998)

The Education Of Little Tree by Forrest Carter, Delacorte Press (1976)

The Field: The Quest For The Secret Force Of The Universe by Lynne McTaggart, Harper Paperbacks (2008)

The Intention Experiment: Using Your Thoughts To Change Your Life And The World by Lynne McTaggart, Free Press (2008)

The Nature Principle: Human Restoration and the End of Nature-Deficit Disorder by Richard Louv, Algonquin Books (2011)

The Other Way to Listen Byrd Baylor, Aladdin (1997)

The Relaxation Response by Herbert Benson, Harpertorch (1975)

The Secret Life Of Plants by Peter Tomkins and Christopher Bird, Penguin Books (1973)

The Seven Spiritual Laws for Parents: Guiding Your Children to Success and Fulfillment by Deepak Chopra, Three Rivers Press (2006)

The Tracker by Tom Brown Jr., Berkley Books (1986)

Tibetan Book of Living And Dying by Sogyal Rinpoche, HarperOne; Revised edition (1994)

Organizations

Wild Earth's Children
Founded by Simon Paul Harrison to re-connect people of all ages with nature and with life.
www.wildearthschildren.org

Tracker School
Tom Brown Jr's Survival, Awareness & Nature School.
So much more than the name suggests, Tom teaches how to develop the deepest connections with nature and with life.
www.trackerschool.com

4 Elements Earth Education
Founded by Rick Berry. Rick is a true visionary who runs the most amazing nature-based programs for children in California.
www.4eee.com

Jon Young
Founder of Wilderness Awareness School, 8 Shields Mentoring. Author of Kamana Naturalist Program and many other great resources for

parents and communities.

Jon.young.org

The Earth-Heart Institute of Vision and Healing.
Malcolm Ringwalt and Allyson Rice offer unique programs for adults to be able to re-connect with who they really are. I highly recommend their programs.

www.visionquest-spiritualretreats-womensretreats-yoga.com/index.htm

Children Of The Earth Foundation
Founded by Tom Brown Jr. to bring his philosophy and teachings to children.

www.cotef.org

Barbara Ann Brennan School of Healing
Provides a fantastic framework in which to become increasingly sensitive to our energy systems and be able to heal and grow.

www.barbarabrennan.com/

Neale Donald Walsch (Author of *Conversations With God*)
Inspiring and thought provoking.

www.nealedonaldwalsch.com/index.php

Lynne McTaggart (Author of *The Field, The Intention Experiment*)
Provides a bridge between science and spirituality.

www.lynnemctaggart.com

Index

About the Author

Simon Paul Harrison was born in England in the small town of North Hykeham, close to Sherwood Forest. While working as an elementary school teacher in London, he developed his vision of supporting the lives of children. Simon had a parting of ways with mainstream education when he moved to the United States to work as the director for The Children of The Earth Foundation, a nonprofit founded and guided by the world-renowned Tom Brown Jr. There he learned the subtle art of Coyote Teaching, a truly remarkable way of mentoring children to become independent learners and lovers of life.

After a number of life-changing years on the east coast, Simon moved to Boulder, Colorado, where he founded Wild Earth's Children. This organization is dedicated to helping children and families to foster deep, meaningful relationships with the Earth through hands-on experiences in nature.

Simon has taught all over North America including Alaska, New England, and the Cree Nation in Quebec, Canada.

He is passionate about the natural world, which he embraces in his programs to further people's connections to life. His favorite thing is simply to sit, be still, and enjoy *being*.

For more information about Wild Earth's Children, visit the website at www.wildearthschildren.org. All donations to this organization are fully tax deductible and are used to bring the messages and experiences in this book to the next generation. We appreciate all forms of support.

You can find and more information on Simon's writing and programs, including blog, videos and audio programs at

www.simonpaulharrison.com.